This book gives its reader permission to be creative, innovative, and wholly authentic in how they start, grow, and scale a business true to their values.

> **PATTY AUBERY**, president of the Canfield Group, cofounder of Chicken Soup for the Soul, and bestselling author of *Permission Granted*

From an early age, Kari Warberg Block developed a strong sense of truth in advertising, and you see her authenticity in every page of this amazing book! From her evolving role as a farmer's wife to that of founder and CEO of a global brand, you'll hear the real story, the real struggles, and the real genius that kept her doggedly pursuing her quest for products that would repel pests like mice and spiders but still be safe around her children and pets. We need more Karis in this world! And you need this book.

> **SHERRY DEUTSCHMANN**, founder and CEO of BrainTrust

Kari is able to capture with great humility the essence of purpose through her farm-to-fortune story. She is able to put into words what she has lived in her life, and she has a great message to students of any age willing to learn. This book is great for those who seek to let opportunities come their way by letting go and letting God. Starting a new chapter in your life? This book is a must-read.

> **DR. KAREL SOVAK**, dean of Gary Tharaldson School of Business, University of Mary

Kari's insightful story of the entrepreneurial journey of building a purpose-driven business based on a passion for nature makes interesting reading for aspiring entrepreneurs. Her life is an example of overcoming seemingly insurmountable challenges with a never-say-die attitude.

G. V. MURALIDHARA, author of the case study "Building a Business from Nature," which won Best Case Award in the Case Centre's "Entrepreneurship" category

Determination. Grit. Kari's story is living proof that if you set your mind to something, you CAN make it happen. We all have doubts and doubters. It's about moving forward and making it all happen. Read this book.

KARA GOLDIN, founder and CEO of Hint, Inc., and author of *Undaunted: Overcoming Doubts and Doubters*

Kari is an old soul with a modern heart. The same way she cares about the earth is the same way she cares about people and all living things. Excited for the world to be inspired by Kari's book Gathering around the Table *and to share in her extraordinary journey of entrepreneurship and passion for sustainability.*

TAMI HOLZMAN, bestselling author of *From C-Student to the C-Suite*, investor, advisor, business coach, and motivational speaker

gathering
around
the table

gathering
around the table

A Story of
Purpose-Driven
Change through
Business

KARI WARBERG BLOCK

with GENEVIEVE V. GEORGET *and* SARAH BYRD

CONSCIOUS
CAPITALISM
PRESS™

Conscious Capitalism Press
www.consciouscapitalism.org/press

Round Table Companies
Packaging, production, and distribution services
www.roundtablecompanies.com

Editors	**Genevieve V. Georget**
	Sarah Byrd
	Mary Anna Rodabaugh
Cover Design	**Christy Bui**
Interior Design	**Christy Bui**
	Sunny DiMartino
Proofreading	**Adam Lawrence**
	Carly Cohen

Printed in the United States of America

First Edition: March 2021
10 9 8 7 6 5 4 3 2 1

Library of Congress Cataloging-in-Publication Data
Gathering around the table: a story of purpose-driven change through business / Kari Warberg Block.—1st ed. p. cm.
ISBN Hardcover: 978-1-950466-20-7
ISBN Paperback: 978-1-950466-21-4
ISBN Digital: 978-1-950466-22-1
Library of Congress Control Number: 2020922238

Conscious Capitalism Press is an imprint of Conscious Capitalism, Inc.
The Conscious Capitalism Press logo is a trademark of Conscious Capitalism, Inc.

Round Table Companies and the RTC logo are trademarks of
Writers of the Round Table, Inc.

Dedicated to Lady Grandma

introduction

I remember the day I woke up to my purpose. Only I didn't know it at the time. It wasn't an angelic, birds singing kind of moment. It burned my eyes, it stung as I inhaled, and it came to me covered in rats and roaches.

It was 1969, shortly after I saw my first television commercial starring a young blond girl who looked just like me, only prettier. She was in the shower washing her hair, wearing a huge smile, and caressing the suds into a crown. As I stared at the television, I realized that I wanted to be that girl, on the other side of the screen, influencing people to buy shampoo that created so much harmony. That commercial was like sugar to my five-year-old palate, and right then I started drinking the Kool-Aid!

My parents bought me the shampoo after relentless and repeated requests. But just like that, my new reality was shattered when the promise given to me by the sweet blond girl was broken. The suds burned my skin, the label yellowed, and the bottle was thrown away. Furthermore, I didn't feel any prettier than before. Every single part of the experience was a total letdown.

That's the moment I became a conscious consumer, wanting to bring everything about a product's brand promise and life cycle into the light. I'd felt so cheated and have carried it within my DNA ever since. I wanted real, through and through. Instead

I got suckered and vowed to never make anyone feel like that as long as I lived. I think that's when my entrepreneur ritual DNA was activated, or at least fertilized with the rich organic matter of compassion.

For a long time afterward, I kept thinking about the disconnect I'd felt after being seduced. I wondered how a company could get away with selling products that burned kids' skin. I wondered, for the first time, if I was pretty enough. And I wondered what happened to the bottles after they were thrown "away."

The first question my mom helped me to navigate.

The second question I didn't dare say out loud.

The third question my father answered like a life scientist only could: by taking me on a short one-and-a-half-hour ride from our apartment in Cherry Hill to Staten Island for a field study of Fresh Kills Landfill, a.k.a. the *Away* or the *Kills Dump*, the nation's largest dumping ground.

1

canary in a coal mine

Sometimes the black sheep is the
only one telling the truth.

—UNKNOWN

I sat cross-legged on my bedroom floor and carefully opened the lid to the cigar box. I did not want to spill the precious contents nestled inside. I grabbed a small piece of string and picked up a tiny mahogany-colored bead. Slowly, I rolled the bead between my fingers, noticing the smooth texture as I inspected it for flaws. Satisfied with my selection, I brushed a lock of blond hair out of my face and threaded the string through the bead with expert precision. I paused for a moment, surveying the choices in the ornate cigar box before choosing a yellow bead to thread next.

I was about nine years old at the time. I continued this meticulous ritual until I completed a beautiful earth-toned bracelet. I tied a knot at the end of the string and set it aside, debating on starting another piece of jewelry. I wanted to complete a few pieces before showing them off for sale. Customers liked options, and I enjoyed making a little money. In fact, I simply enjoyed making things.

When I wasn't crafting under the watchful eye of my oversized cat poster, you could find me scouring the ground in Washington or the farmlands of North Dakota for arrowheads, foraging for herbs, or tending to plants. I was described by some as an odd child, entranced by nature and everything it had to offer. I tried to assimilate into the childhood joys of play and adventure. I wanted to participate in "boy sports" like hockey, but the boys would never let girls play. I wanted to join the swim team, but my parents couldn't make the schedules work, nor could they afford it. When I wanted to try ballet and tap dancing, I was told the same thing: "We can't afford that, Kari."

Instead I found solace on the playground. I loved climbing the monkey bars. I would sit on the grass and trace the textures of dirt with my fingers, feeling a connection with Earth in a way my young mind couldn't quite understand just yet. When other kids chased each other, screaming in delight, I sat quietly, listening to the way the wind danced through the trees.

I did these things and felt these things ever since my father took me to the Away. I remember at five years old experiencing that deep pain when I realized I was very connected to the planet. My heart hurt for those women and children working to find "treasures" in the garbage to sell on a tin table leaning on the packed dirt covered in trash. My soul hurt for the earth burdened by all the waste piled on top of its glorious soil. As I got a little older, I started making very conscious choices. I refused to throw plastic bottles away. I knew where they ended up, and I knew the people who would rummage through rubbish to collect them.

My parents would use Tupperware to store food and serve meals on plastic plates. Some may call me a petulant child, but I refused to eat off the plastic. I requested a stoneware dish instead. I wanted to eat off something made from the earth. Despite our hand-me-down clothes and shoestring budget, my parents, like the shampoo bottle request, obliged. Besides, a stoneware plate cost much less than ballet lessons.

I was born in Logan, Utah, in 1963. My parents were basically children when they got married. My mom was one of eight kids, most of whom had bouts of alcoholism, with the exception of my mother. She wanted a way out, and my father was it. They were still in college when my mom got pregnant with me. My father actually showed me the exact spot on a country road where "my seed was planted." They were young and in love. And two years later, my sister Kim came along. My father got an entomology degree and was just one credit short of a PhD. My mother was a teacher. They were good people, but beyond their jobs, they never really saw themselves as being of service to others. At least not during my early years. Instead, I looked out for my little sister when they couldn't afford a babysitter, causing my nurturing side to blossom at a very young age.

I remember when I signed my mom up to be a Girl Scouts troop leader once. I aspired to get every badge on the sash that I could. I loved learning, the outdoors, and using the environment to create things. It was a perfect fit. I didn't mind the ranger green dress if it meant I could learn and be tested on practical survival skills. But it wasn't a good fit for my mom. While my mother loved me, she was more of a hands-off parent. So she rejected my nomination of her as troop leader. I wanted so desperately for her to like it. I wanted to have something that I could share with her. Disappointed, I gave up and quit Girl Scouts. From that day forward I did not ask my parents for a single thing. It was mutual. They didn't ask anything of me either.

We moved around a lot. I've lived in Utah, Idaho, Minnesota, Washington, New Jersey, and North Dakota, just to name a few. My father worked tirelessly to climb the career ladder. He was driven, to say the least. My father's love for nature and disgust for being "chained to a desk" as a pencil pusher served as a key motivator in his life. He eventually bought a Shell gas station in Minnesota. One gas station turned into a chain of forty-plus gas stations, which meant we were in constant change as a family.

I didn't have the opportunity to make lasting friendships, but I didn't care to either. I was fine by myself, finding animals to observe or working on crafts like the beaded bracelet next to my feet. I liked to explore and discover and followed the path my curiosities seemed to ignite. I could lose myself in the wonder of encyclopedias just as I could spend hours roaming the fragrant and earthy aisles of health food stores. We didn't have many health food stores growing up, but anytime I found one, I spent plenty of my time and money in it to formulate every kind of remedy needed.

I was happiest outdoors or while listening to music. I loved Rick James. When I was ten years old, I joined a music club without my parents knowing. I signed a deal where I had to buy albums each month. At the time, I had a paper route, which allowed me to make my own money. Since I was never hung up on material things, I saved up so I could afford my monthly music and avoid a parental chastisement.

I loathed school. I didn't understand what people liked about being confined in chairs all day while people talked at you. It felt like a prison. I'd stare wishfully out the window and wonder what the Earth was up to. Naturally, my grades reflected my distaste for school. I was always behind, always withdrawn, always the last kid picked for the team. I was also in special education, so that did not help with the social bounty school is supposed to provide. Despite what the school system might have said, I didn't really have a learning disability as much as I had an inability to want to cooperate in formal educational settings. It didn't seem to matter much, though, because my parents never checked my report card, so I did not have "dire consequences" motivating me to do better.

There was one time in school when I brought in The Alan Parsons Project's "The Raven" from their *Tales of Mystery and Imagination* album. This song complemented my book report on Poe's work beautifully. I loved their musical take on classic stories. It was raw, original, and at times haunting. I stood in front of the class and played a selection only to be stopped mid-presentation. My classmates thought I was a freak. My teacher didn't see the genius of these artists and their music either. I was told to go back to my seat. Even as a child, I sought deeper experiences and truths beyond what was merely presented.

It was always like this. Me constantly on a different level than my teachers and peers, and the educational institution trying to teach me what was "proper." At the end of each school day, though, I'd be released back into the world, a place where I knew I belonged. Upon reaching my doorstep, I'd pull out the gold key tied around my neck by a piece of yellow yarn and unlock the front door.

I'd check on my plants before deciding what I'd like to do until my parents returned home.

I went to a different school every year of my life until ninth grade. My nickname was "Kari Convict." I guess people thought I'd steal things? I never really understood that label. I never stole. Forage? Yes, but I gathered natural things such as stones, seeds, fruits, and flowers. And most people didn't really know about that part of my life.

Like the sea, we just ebbed and flowed in our own rhythm. Sometimes with force and other times with tranquility, but always moving, always shifting. To say my life was always changing is an understatement. But the biggest change hit us like a crashing wave drowning a nearby shore.

When my mother was a child, she had rheumatic fever and it damaged her heart. As an adult, she had about six strokes, each one more terrifying than the next. During one particular hospital visit, the doctor said she needed emergency surgery. My father kissed her lips before they wheeled her into the operating room.

My sister and I didn't know what was happening. My father's mother, Grandma Dorothy, (though I used to call her Lady Grandma), quickly made her way to pick us up from our friend's home where we had been staying separately. As soon as we collected together again as a family, our pastor stopped by the house. As he walked through our front door, with a look of despair across his face, I realized I would never see my mother again. And while we weren't always close, she was still my mother, and her leaving me sooner than I expected was too much.

"How long has she been dead?" I screamed. "How long?"

I was only eleven, but even then, I knew someone should have told us.

"Your father wanted to tell you, but he just couldn't. I'm so sorry for your loss," the pastor said to me.

I turned on my heel and ran up the stairs to the second floor of our house. Tears burned my eyes as I flung open my bedroom window and began to mount the ledge. I stared down at the grass and prepared to jump. I wanted to join my mother. Thankfully, I didn't. I paused, put my emotions aside for a quick moment, and decided I would probably just end up breaking my leg. I climbed back down and closed the window, falling to my floor in a heap of sadness.

It turns out that my mother suffered a brain aneurysm during surgery. She was in a coma on life support afterward, and my father had to make the horrifying but necessary choice to pull the plug. She was only thirty-three years old. My father was never the same again.

I think my mother knew she was going to die. A week or so later, we found boxes of her possessions packed up in the basement, carefully labeled with black marker on masking tape. Her whole life was tucked neatly away, and we never suspected a thing when she was alive. Sure, the strokes were scary, but no one in our family assumed the worst was right around the corner.

Our whole family was a wreck. Everyone felt broken, and I was determined to fix it. I felt powerless and helpless, and I wanted to ease my own grief by doing something nice for everyone else. If I could lessen their pain, maybe my own would drop down a degree and I could make sense of this enormous loss.

Knowing I liked to collect things, Lady Grandma would give

me antique coins. After a few years, I had an impressive collection. Some of the treasures dated back to the 1800s. I wasn't into dolls or toys or material things. When I received a gift such as these coins, I took care of it. But my heart ached. It ached like it did that day I saw the Away. Everyone around me was drowning in grief and turmoil after my mother passed. Instead of joining in on the sadness, I racked my brain on how to make everyone feel better again.

A few days later it came to me. As I played with the antique coins, I realized they were worth something. I could trade them for money and buy everyone presents. Then they would feel a little better and I could establish order, peace, and maybe even a sense of healing in the household. I put the coins in one of my favorite boxes and set off to the local bank.

With everything carefully tucked under my arm, I carefully opened the bank's front door and walked inside. I found an open teller and popped the box onto the counter.

"I want to trade these in for cash. They're very valuable," I said confidently.

The teller stood up from her chair and peered over the counter, looking down at my hopeful eyes and favorite box filled with treasure.

"Let me take a look," she said curtly.

I stood there and waited, plotting out the gifts I wanted to buy my dad, my sister, and my grandparents. Surely this would fix everything. The teller reached across the counter and slid my box onto her side of the window. Moments later she returned.

"I can give you $37.50. That's face value for the lot," she said.

"You have a deal," I replied without hesitation. She slapped the money on the counter with a smile—I would only realize many years later—of someone who had just conned an eleven-year-old girl out of valuable antique coins that would only increase in worth.

"Have a great day," she said.

Money in hand, I set off to buy the presents. That evening I triumphantly bestowed my gifts upon my family. Everyone was happy, even just for a moment. Well, almost everyone. My grandmother knew how I got the money to pull off this grand surprise, and she felt horrible. On the one hand, she was disappointed, but on the other hand, she felt guilty that I felt the need to sell precious possessions to cheer everyone up. I didn't regret it. The caregiver within me was satisfied.

After my mother died, we sold everything and moved to Williston, North Dakota. My aunt and uncle helped us get back on our feet. My father worked at a gas station next to a bar. He would walk over to the bar on his lunch breaks, most likely to have a drink, as he had been self-medicating since my mother's death. He ended up meeting Paulette at that bar and eventually married her. She had a less-than-desirable reputation in the small town, but my father didn't care. My sister and I were not sure what my father saw in her. She wasn't warm or loving or even helpful to us, unless it involved making us into her version of social elite. She loved status and craved to be rich one day. Why she married the owner of a bunch of gas stations was beyond me. I later found out she was a gold digger and hoped my father would make her rich as his business grew.

I quietly watched her and understood she would do anything for the "status" of being rich and well known. She always remarked on the "things" people had, like fancy clothes and cars. She never spoke about who a person *was* but rather what a person *had*. Those observations helped me develop my own sense of humility and a desire to be valued for contribution rather than my body, looks, or family money. I think when you strive to be seen for material possessions or physical attributes, it's all too easy to lose your self-confidence, to cling desperately to a distorted idea of what it means to be valued in this world. When all was said and done, I think Paulette was afraid of being too normal.

Speaking of fear, it's not something I really experienced much as a child. With one exception. The only time I really felt it was when I was walking to and from school. I was fearful I would get lost. Even if the school was only a block from my house, I'd meticulously map out my route so I didn't make a wrong turn. To this day, I still do that when I travel.

I learned at a young age that I could figure out anything I needed to, and I worked with the environment to get it. I credit Lady Grandma for that. Despite this confidence, I still didn't think I was good at anything. Unlike other kids my age, I never aspired to be anything when I grew up. I didn't have many role models. I just focused on making it through each family move and, as the inspirational saying goes, attempted to bloom wherever I was planted.

Sometimes, though, I was the brightest, most exotic flower in the bunch. By ninth grade, I finally would attend the same school for four years: high school, in Williston, North Dakota. Always wanting to try something new, I decided I wanted to be a cheerleader. It would be physically demanding, I might make friends, and I could set some personal goals for myself in the process. I tried out in ninth grade, and while I did not make the main team, I did score the role of alternate. So if one of the girls got sick or injured, I could quickly step in and flawlessly take their place.

Except cheerleading was much like the fantasy world my stepmother lived in. I quickly caught on to the politics involved, and the club antics were nothing I wanted to be a part of. The girls collectively decided who we could hang out with, who we could date, and even what we could wear. They wore matching dresses to prom in preapproved coordinating colors. Sheep mentality at its finest. No, thank you.

One of my teammates' boyfriends even told me about the unspoken "rules" one day. Classic Mean Girls. The poor guy's dates were all based on the squad's collective decisions. His girlfriend's friends had to know everything, all the time, about their relationship. While I appreciated the intel, word got back to "the squad" that a "taken" boyfriend was speaking to me. I guess that conversation was not sanctioned. The girls were extra catty toward me after that. All I did was have a conversation with the guy, but the peer torment was enough to make me swear off dating a schoolmate after that. I didn't even want to associate with my peers. I spent my free time hanging out with a few people outside of school.

I actually got permission to bring my twenty-year-old friend from Costa Rica to prom. The principle agreed and everything. What a spectacle that was! He was gay and colorful, like an uninhibited wildflower. I did not care what others thought. I knew I wanted to try the prom thing at least once, on my own terms. I met

11

Carlos at the Ramada Inn, where I worked as a desk clerk after school. He was a bartender who taught me how to speak Spanish and play beach soccer. When I worked a three-to-eleven shift without a break, Carlos would bring me virgin piña coladas. He'd even help me with chores and paint my nails. I'm glad I got to give him an American prom experience and was equally pleased by the bewildered reactions from my peers, who called him a pimp, and teachers, who called him a wetback.

Little did I know that my earliest experiences would have a profound effect on my future and the life I live today. I had no idea that a shampoo commercial would awaken an environmentally conscious beast within my soul. I had no idea my upbringing would foster such a strong streak of independence (and later translate into invaluable leadership skills). I never knew my ability to "march to the beat of my own drum" would later be seen as an inspiration and desirable trait among women in business. Above all, I could have never predicted that my trust in the environment to provide me with solutions to any problem I faced would eventually lead me down a path to starting and running a multimillion-dollar pest control product line. Mother Nature is certainly full of gifts, isn't she?

Sometimes we have no control where we are planted. We just have to look around, see what resources we can use in the moment, and flourish against all odds.

2

an ode to lil' hustlers

The dream is free. The hustle is sold separately.

—TYRESE GIBSON

Our family was never rich by any means. My father did well for himself, but that did not translate into an abundance of material goods or expensive experiences for our family. Money and I had an interesting relationship. I was resourceful and loved making money. However, I didn't love making money for the same reasons most other people loved making money: to buy things, to have status, to be able to do whatever they wanted to do. No, I loved making money because I loved investing it into making other things, such as gifts, bath products, and natural anointments (concoctions, as Lady Grandma called them). I loved money because I love to create and bless.

Which is why it is no surprise that at the young age of six, I decided it was time to go through every child entrepreneur's rite of passage: a front-step lemonade stand. My family and I were living in Cherry Hill, New Jersey, in a high-rise apartment at the time. I was only in kindergarten, but I knew it was an easy way to make a few dollars on a hot afternoon. Except I didn't take the easy route on this one. I seldom ever did. Instead of mixing some packaged powder and water in a pitcher, I talked my mom into purchasing a few ripe lemons and asked my parents if I could use a strainer and a little sugar. My lemonade was fresh-squeezed and authentic. I sold this real lemonade at a higher cost to the moms in the high-rise, while the other two kids sold the cheap imitation version. Even at that age, I knew how to make natural products and sell them. I also knew the importance of selling exactly what you advertise and nothing less. That lesson came to me the hard way from that yellow shampoo bottle months earlier.

I was always scheming as a child. When I wasn't drawing, listening to music, or spending as much time as possible outdoors, I was coming up with new business ideas. When I went to visit my grandfather in the Turtle Mountains of North Dakota, I would spend hours combing through the farmland looking for unique animal bones. It was quite a treasure hunt. I wanted to collect a large batch of bones and clean them off, making them shiny and white again. When my grandfather caught on to what I was doing, he was a bit perturbed.

"What are you gonna do with all those bones, Kari?" he asked.

"Well, I'm going to bleach them, log them, number them, pack them up, and bring them back to the city to sell to my friends on the East Coast," I replied confidently.

"Who on earth wants some old animal bones?"

"You know how people say you can hear the ocean when you

hold a seashell up to your ear? Well, I'm going to tell my customers you can hear the ancient buffalo of the prairie by listening to these curated artifacts. You know, like people do with seashells to hear the ocean. I know I can sell the lot, and some people will collect them."

My grandfather let out a hardy laugh. He couldn't believe the stuff my six-year-old mind came up with. Unfortunately, my brilliant idea didn't come to fruition. My dad got wind of my plan and put the brakes on it. He said the Department of Agriculture would have to get involved and something like little girls and bleach don't mix. Apparently, it was a "safety and regulatory issue." He gave me credit for having such an ingenious idea, though.

Given that I was so devout in my business authenticity at such a young age, you might suspect this endeavor to be a bit of a scam. I didn't think it was false advertising, though. Even if the bones did not come from wild buffalo, we all evolved from various animals, right? I bet a bit of each animal's spirit is passed onto the next generation of evolution. Besides, animal bones looked really cool. It would have been an easy sell.

Since I wasn't allowed to use the bleach and transport the numbered bones, I defaulted back to my old system of collecting arrowheads along the streams, where the early Native Americans used to hunt, until I had enough to take to a museum to authenticate and sell. My cousin had an expert eye and could spot the tip of a rogue arrowhead hidden under a clump of grass, or mud, with ease. We made a good team.

I didn't always have to create my own schemes, though. Back when I lived in Eagan, Minnesota, on Yankee Doodle Road, I worked as a neighborhood paper girl. I quickly learned that the physical aspects of hurling papers at doors ridiculously early in the morning were not for me, especially in the frigid cold and dark of Minnesota in the winter. I had to figure out a way to make money but avoid the not-so-great aspects of the job. After a little brainstorming, I had a brand-new idea. My plan was to convince the neighborhood boys to join forces with me; I would pay them a small portion to take my route and deliver papers, and I would handle the arduous task of collecting subscription fees from customers.

As it turns out, the boys hated that part of the job, so it was an easy negotiation. I'd go door to door (at a far more reasonable hour) and let customers know how much they owed. With an outstretched hand, I'd ask them to "pay up." If you think it would be hard to resist an adorable little girl with blond locks standing innocently on your doorstep, then you'd be wrong. Customers would lie to me. They'd say they paid last week or that they would pay me next week. I had doors slammed right in my face. People were mean. It was a hard job, and it made me wonder if waking up early wasn't so bad after all.

I hated being cheated, but I didn't have an issue with the confrontation. I was there to do a job, and that was it. Little did I know that this employment experience would prepare me for a lifetime of negotiation. I liked working and keeping busy. I enjoyed my pay day when I could purchase materials to make things like flower baskets or natural medicinal remedies. Looking back, I'd say the whole gig was worth every slammed door. During this same time, I was an official and bright-orange-sashed bus patrol. I'm still not 100 percent sure that the driver didn't make me wear the sash to keep a closer eye on me after I was beat up a few times. Not only was I one of the only white kids in the neighborhood, but I had a challenging way about me when I saw small children being bullied.

By the time I reached high school, I worked at a country kitchen, a KFC, and as a desk clerk at a nearby Ramada Inn. Impressed with my drive, my father hired me to work at his gas station. I started out as a bookkeeper, tracking the financial aspects of our day-to-day business. Eventually my father also had me help with collections of all things. A little bit older and wiser, I kept track of what customers owed us.

Working with my father created a bond usually reserved for daughters and fathers at a much older age: the bond of business. I remember looking up at a sign above the door of his first gas station in North Dakota. It read "John Havnvik—Owner/Operator." At the time I wondered what that meant. I looked at my dad, in his blue pants with battery-acid holes and oil stains spattered on the front, and an untucked Standard Oil blue polo shirt. He looked like one of the mechanics. In a way, he was. My father was always hands-on. He'd change tires, pump fuel, and meticulously wash windshields. He wouldn't stop until everything was perfect. Compulsively perfect.

He always had a way of looking approachable. It may have been his huge smile or perhaps his blue, sparkly Paul Newman eyes. The ladies used to swoon over him, something my sister and I really didn't understand. My father took everything to a whole new level with his people and his customers. For example, he made it a rule that all of his staff had to greet customers in the eyes—with an authentic smile—within one minute of the customer's arrival. He loved to see people happy and delighted.

It was a simple business lesson, but one I carried with me throughout my life. When we lived in New Jersey, we'd ride the subway and people wouldn't look you in the eye. When I moved out west, my teachers would tell me to look them in the eye when talking to them. As a bit of an introvert, I found greeting people with an honest smile and eye contact to be uncomfortable. I really had to learn to greet people with my heart instead of business as usual. I learned how to see people through their eyes and soul before their bodies. By seeing the heart of people, I could also see their potential. Or their intention to never pay their bill. I believe that lesson was one of the keys to my father's success. I used to listen in on my father's business conversations because I found them so fascinating.

Some talks were really entertaining. I remember one day my father said he was going to list his company on the Nasdaq. "The day it's official, I'm going to walk down Wall Street, and I'm going to quack like a duck, and I'm gonna do it in my underwear," he said. I laughed and looked at him like he must be kidding. At that very moment, he perched upon his desk and jumped down onto the floor, lifting his elbows up and down and quacking like a duck. The people in the office were working like it was nothing out of the normal. I laughed so hard and can hear it to this day.

With his genuine enthusiasm for the job and meticulous work ethic, my father became quite successful. Eventually the gas station in North Dakota broke records for sales. What started as "I'm just going to pump some gas and be happy about it" attitude eventually gave way to my father's inner entrepreneurial drive. He wanted to branch out and purchase multiple gas stations to start a convenience store chain.

For my father, this wasn't just a business. These were people. First and foremost. And he believed that the best way to take care of the business was by taking care of its people. He planned to put large canopies over the gas pumps and install plenty of lighting so women would feel safe pumping gas, day or night. In a time when gas stations were notorious for never having clean bathrooms, my father ensured that his were. It was a standard in all his stores that the bathrooms were well-lit and cleaned every hour. He felt that strangers should be treated as good as family. He'd say we are all one family; clean bathrooms and greeting people with a smile will help us remember that.

He also sold eggs and milk at the same price as the local supermarket, allowing families a chance to pump their gas and pick up basic groceries too. He'd tell me the margins were thin on gas, that he made all his money at the checkout with impulse items. When it came time to name the future chain, he asked for my help. Together, we came up with the name "Superpumper" and a logo. I didn't know it at the time, but I had some innate marketing skills in that busy little mind of mine.

I was good at many things. Not school, of course, or sports, but more worldly things. I was good at noticing the unnoticed and recognizing someone's potential. In high school, I used to cross the street and talk to the "burnout" kids about their futures. These were the kids who skipped class and were labeled as "problem students" by the administration. I'd try to find them odd jobs like dishwashing or delivering newspapers to help them out. These kids were "the forgotten." Perhaps they were a human version of the Away, and no one seemed to notice them. I'm sure people thought I was weird, associating with those kids, but I never lived my life based on what other people thought of me. (My sister admitted to me years later that I scared her by associating with these kids, and she was equally as embarrassed when I wore my knee-high beaded moccasins in public.)

While I didn't make money to buy material possessions, there was one thing that I couldn't wait to get my hands on. It was beautiful, it was white, and it represented the freedom and independence I had always craved. It was a '73 Mustang Grande. I was seventeen at the time, and after months of carefully budgeting and saving, I purchased my first car and fixed it up really nice. I paid for a lift kit, nice tires, and to have it painted with metal flakes in it. I wanted it white, and when it was parked under a light, it would glisten like a star. It had a celery-green interior because it had to be green like nature. And a stereo, it needed a really good stereo. As much as I enjoyed riding my bike, my car let me get to places much quicker, which meant I could even work more jobs if I wanted.

I had extra time to save up for this car because I didn't get my license like most other kids in my town: at fifteen years old, after passing drivers ed. My driving instructor called me a "damn woman driver" when the golf ball came off the tee in the back window.

"You can't talk to me like that!" I told him.

"Yes, I can, and I just did. You women are all alike," he replied, without hesitation.

I confidently got out of the car while he reminded me that if he didn't sign my certificate—which he wasn't prepared to do if I left—then I wouldn't get my license until I was sixteen. I walked miles home that day and told the principal in the morning. The driving instructor never spoke to a student like that again. I guess no one else dared to call him on it. Quite a few girls who had also done drivers training thanked me afterward for taking one for the team.

When I was sixteen, my stepmother sat me down and said, "When you turn eighteen, you are out of this house, so you best start thinking about it now." I likely would have left without needing the nudge ahead of time, but now knowing that there was a family consensus, I worked tirelessly to save money. My car was paid off by the time I graduated high school. And though I had every intention of bolting from my house the day of my birthday, wanting so badly to make it out on my own, it turns out I had no idea how ill-prepared I really was.

Growing up, I never found myself with future aspirations. My friends wanted to be dental hygienists or teachers or flight attendants. It wasn't that I didn't want to be *anything*; I just didn't want to be a specific *something*. I think it was less about a lack of ambition and more about my keen ability to stay present in the moment. I wasn't futuristic, although futurism was my favorite class. Saving money to move out was about as futuristic as I had ever been up to this point.

After graduation, I had to figure out what to do with myself. A big fancy college was out of the picture. I didn't have the tuition, and I didn't have the grades. Despite this, I still wanted a change of scenery. I saved up enough money to afford tuition at a hotel restaurant management vocational school in Bismarck, North Dakota, about four hours from Williston. It was a logical choice given all my experience working in hotels. Best of all, I could afford it and I didn't need an SAT to get in. I enrolled in the program and eleven months later earned my Hotel, Motel, and Restaurant Management certificate. I graduated second in my class. I learned a lot about management in general, but my classes took a "food science" turn that I wasn't quite expecting. I wasn't very interested in that at the time, so I didn't continue the program beyond my certification.

I called my dad to tell him the program wasn't quite working out the way I had hoped. "Well, Kari, what do you want to do?" he asked me.

"I want to develop people. I want to work in human resources," I told him.

"That's the most difficult job in a company and even harder to get into," my dad said.

"What about with your company? Maybe I could study human resources and, in a few years, take on an HR role for you?" I suggested.

"No, sorry, Kari. We don't need another HR person. I can't help you. You have to figure it out," he told me.

I had never felt so rejected in my life. I didn't have a purpose. I didn't have a plan. I didn't have friends. I wondered if I was any good to anybody. And I started to hate myself. I was paralyzed and didn't know what the next step would be and subsequently tumbled into a deep depression.

The hardest hours of the day came between four p.m. and six p.m. I called it my darkness hours. The sun would be going down, and the darkness would envelope me. I became bulimic, using food as a comfort, only to purge it shortly after consumption. This went on for quite some time, until one day I forced myself to stop.

I cried out, loudly, in my little apartment on the top floor of a house. I begged God for help. It was my only lifeline at the time. As I sat there with tears streaming down my face, I cried out the pent-up grief I had never fully released for my mother. I cried out the pain and rejection I felt on a daily basis. I cried out my fear over living alone in a world without the means to navigate it.

Eventually, my tears subsided, and my breathing returned to normal. At that moment it was as if a light switch went off. I had to quit being so mean to myself. I was special because God loved me. That was enough. That was all I needed at that moment. I picked myself up and vowed to get healthier.

I would no longer see food as the enemy. I would no longer use my own words as weapons. I would no longer allow my past or the people in it to define me. I rose from that floor into an understanding that my life was mine to create. Today. Tomorrow. Always.

Alone in the world with a single certificate to show for it, I did something I never thought I'd do: I humbly returned back home to Williston, the very place I couldn't wait to leave. Instead of wallowing in defeat, I began to brainstorm my next big business idea, which turned out to be a balloon-delivery and singing-telegram service called "Balloon Greetings."

Customers would call to place an order for a specific occasion. I filled earthen terracotta pots with colorful floral wrapping, added French candies, and affixed a bunch of balloons to the pots. I hired my friends to deliver them in cute logoed red jumpsuits.

My stepmother, Paulette, ended up opening a shop downtown called "Treasure Island Gifts." I sold my candy balloon grams to her until the shop failed. She ended up doing some balloon decorating for events in town on the side. Ever the entrepreneur, I had other means of income aside from "Balloon Greetings." I worked as a hotel desk clerk in the evenings and began saving up again for my next move.

I never gave up. That is the beauty of not having a specific career in mind as you grow up. You completely avoid the risk of failure. You dodge your own personal expectations simply because you don't have any. I'm not sure anyone expected anything out of me since I was such a wild child, going wherever the breeze carried me. I followed the opportunities wherever they led and made my own opportunities when the existing ones were not enough.

I was accustomed to moving around every few years. Despite wanting to plant myself in the same place for a period of time, my burning desire to leave Williston returned. I made a big leap and set off to Minneapolis. Maybe city life was for me. For the first time in a long time, I took it easy. I laid by the hotel pool during the day and worked at the beautiful Mexican hotel, Granada Royal, as a desk clerk during the rest of my free time. Naturally I got bored quickly. I wasn't sure what I'd do next until I found a housekeeping ad in the paper for a property near East Glacier Park, Montana. It would be a one-way ticket out of the city and put me back near nature where I knew I belonged. Whenever I strayed too far from nature, she had a way of calling me back. My restlessness and boredom were always a sign.

In the spring of 1983, I packed up my things and moved to East

Glacier Park. It isn't exactly a park, just in case you were wondering. It is really a quaint village situated between majestic mountains. It is surrounded by waterfalls, lakes, streams, and plenty of wildlife. Best of all, it was truly "off the grid." There were no banks or pharmacies, beauty salons, or even bars. I loved the simplicity of it all.

My new post involved working for a couple who leased St. Mary's Lodge near the east entrance to Glacier Park. I cleaned rooms and tended to private guests. I didn't mind lugging the seventy-pound cart up the jagged hills to the private cabins where Willie Nelson and other celebrities came in by private helicopter. My coworker was there training for the Olympics, and we both loved the natural solitude and physical exertion required of the role. I planned to stay at the lodge over the winter and write.

My love for writing began when I had to complete a ten-page typed paper on the topic of boredom in high school. My teacher flipped out after reading my first sentence: "Boredom is the lack of capacity for registering subtle vibrations." It was my first taste of freewriting, and it felt phenomenal. I hoped this new employment opportunity would give me plenty of time to indulge in this love. I find my writing always brings me to some sort of change, either internally or externally. Writing forces me to turn myself inside out. It is almost like I hear something with my left ear and write it with my right hand. The whole process is akin to unearthing new treasures.

When I wasn't writing, I knew I could work at the local grocery store and enjoy the solitude the little village had to offer. I ended up changing my mind at the last minute after a reality check from my employers. During the offseason, they told me it would be me and a few Blackfoot Native Americans hanging out over winter. This specific group was known for their drinking, and sometimes liked to shoot stuff up. Not the best place for a single girl to spend a cold winter alone.

As autumn came to a close, I packed up my things once again and went to see my grandma in Belfield, North Dakota. I was headed to Scottsdale, Arizona, for a group tour guide job at the Marriott Camelback. Just as I answered the call for a new adventure, I also answered a call deep in my heart. I needed my grandmother, and, in a way, I think she needed me too. I enjoyed her company. I loved to watch her eat her oatmeal in the morning with her Bible in one hand. She would give me sound life advice that I desperately needed. I passed up on the Arizona job and moved two hours away to Bismarck, where I had first attended college, so I could be closer to my grandmother. After a little bit of searching, I found a job as a waitress. I also paid homage to my childhood roots and delivered newspapers during the early morning hours and worked as a bookkeeper and collector.

My heart led the way. Not only did I get to be closer to my grandmother, but I also landed in a company that would forever change my life. A whole new chapter of my life began.

Sometimes opportunities find their way to you. Other times, you have to create your own opportunity. But regardless of whether you step out on the path knowing exactly where you want to go, or whether you allow the path to unfold before you, when you live in the moment and practice unrelenting determination, you will end up exactly where you are meant to be.

3

semblance of adulting

> *A rising tide lifts all the boats.*
> —JOHN F. KENNEDY

I was working multiple jobs in North Dakota, still trying to figure out what mark I was supposed to leave on the world, when my car at the time—a yellow Volkswagen Beetle—needed some work. The only Volkswagen Audi shop in the small town was closed. A few people recommended a "backyard mechanic" who could do the job and within my budget. I brought my car to him, and as he meticulously examined the vehicle, I could tell he was kind. There was a strong sense of compassion about him. It may have been in his eyes, or the way he assured me we'd get to the root of my car troubles, but whatever it was, it interested me.

I learned that when he wasn't fixing up cars, he worked at a junkyard and also delivered newspapers. Apparently, the art of delivering papers wasn't done with me yet. He started to help me with the odd task here or there, and I, in turn, helped him. The nurturer deep within me was ignited again, and we began a symbiotic relationship. We ended up moving into a trailer together to save both of us money.

As he graduated to the role of "male roommate," and, well—for the sake of clarity—my boyfriend, I used that term loosely. It was an interesting time for me. I did not have much self-confidence by way of looks, as I recovered from my bulimia. There wasn't much of a sexual spark between us; it was more of a cohabitation/mutual assistance situation, but it was nice to have someone around. Someone to share space with. I thought this is what adults do. They attract other people and build lives together.

I was working as a waitress at the time and picked up a few other odd jobs. Craving stability and financial security, I searched for a better part-time job. I figured if I could land a spot in retail, I could also get discounts on clothing, which would help save money. I poured over newspaper ads and asked around town, until one day I found an ad for a sales position with Dayton Hudson Corporation (now known as Target).

When I went in for my interview, they asked me to be a counter manager for Georgios of Beverly Hills. It would have been a really good job, but I just couldn't see myself at a cosmetic counter selling perfumes. Having turned down the opportunity, I thought I blew my chances with the company. That is, until a few weeks later they called me again and asked me how I'd feel about selling shoes for commission. Now that was something in my wheelhouse. Back in high school I also worked at a department store selling shoes part time. With an enthusiastic "yes," I began the start of a really good job with an exceptional corporation.

Every morning, when I walked through the front door, I'd be greeted by roaring music and a huge hug (not the creepy kind) from my boss, Randy. I loved and appreciated the music, but I wasn't exactly a fan of the hugs. He told me, "One day you will get used to this." Regardless, Randy was the type of store manager who wanted to nurture people's skills and watch them grow. If I had an idea that would increase sales, he encouraged my supervisor to let me run with it. If I ran into a problem, he was supportive and helped us solve it. He and my supervisor were the best bosses I could have asked for. My part-time commission role grew into a full-time position. I got benefits for the first time in my life and started to see real career possibilities.

The art of shoe sales requires intuition. I'd read my customers, start a friendly conversation, and determine through my interactions what they liked and didn't like. I always brought four pairs of shoes out so they would have options. It was such a rush when I helped customers feel good about themselves. My sales intuition and ability to connect with customers did not go unnoticed. Dayton Hudson needed someone at the Lancôme counter and told me I was a perfect fit.

I didn't think so at the time though. Perfume, cosmetics, chemicals: it was not my thing. However, they assured me it was technical sales, meaning I'd instruct people and educate them how to use the makeup. I didn't even wear makeup, but I'd get free samples, and it was an opportunity to test out new skills. After training in Minneapolis and a series of makeup lessons from my coworkers, I found myself at the makeup counter conducting elegant makeovers that accentuated each woman's natural beauty instead of showcasing a thick cosmetic mask. My natural approach led to more sales. I enjoyed helping people love themselves more. After all, I was also learning how to love myself.

There were only two problems with selling the makeup. For starters, the sales competition could be a bit ego-driven. Instead of selling products that were best for the customer, there was a competitive aura in the air, and girls would try to sell the most expensive products. The second issue was the perfume that surrounded the cosmetics. I would get such a headache after hours of makeovers and good conversation. The fragrance was dizzying. It got to the point where I had to leave and find something else.

My Dayton Hudson career did not end there, though. The company was so into training and development, which happened to be one of my greatest joys in life, and I continued to be watered and appreciated. The empowerment fostered by the leadership led me to raise my hand for many things. I volunteered for committees, training modules, and unofficial leadership roles. They were the first company to give me paid vacation. I bought stock with them. And, I would soon learn, they put family first.

My life had purpose. I could feel it in my bones. I helped develop and train the staff. I helped customers discover self-love. I finally felt like I was on my own in the world, working toward a great career. With that part of my life seeming to align, my life blossomed in other ways as well. My roommate/boyfriend proposed, and I accepted. I figured adults get married, so this was something I had to do. Granted, I put off the wedding three times, but still. Eventually, one thing led to another, and on June 7, 1988, I gave birth to our son, John.

Childbirth was a harrowing experience. I had to be induced because I should have delivered much earlier, and complications arose. When the doctor checked on me, he was horrified to find I had basically prolapsed. Delivery was terrifying and traumatic, as the doctor screamed and cursed, frantically trying to deliver my son and keep me alive. While I was thrilled to bring a beautiful new and healthy life into the world, albeit with a permanent head scar from the forceps experience, I vowed that day I would never get pregnant again. Childbirth was not for me.

When John and I returned home from the hospital, I found the back door to the deck wide open. My husband and I would usually leave it open for the dog to come in and out of the yard. As I crossed the threshold into the house, I was stunned. Our dog had tracked mud and dirt into the house from room to room. Before I left to deliver, I intentionally made the house immaculate and baby-ready. I had every surface cleaned and every corner organized. With trepidation, I walked through the rooms to find more disarray. My husband was upstairs wreaking havoc with his shell-reloading station, which is like a self-serve ice-cream sundae bar, except it's full of rifle and shotgun shells, tiny pellets, and gun powder. Not exactly the items you want your babies exposed to. The house was a mess.

At that moment I knew my marriage was over. It was far more than a messy house or muddy pawprints on the floor. It became obvious to me that my husband did not want to take responsibility as a parent and that our priorities were in deep misalignment.

As I adjusted to the first week of motherhood and my newfound realization that my marriage was nearing an end after barely having begun, my husband and I tried out a little post-pregnancy intimacy. Perhaps it could help clear my doubts. Instead, it did something else.

I went in for my ten-day checkup with my doctor and said, "I think I'm pregnant."

"There is no way, Kari. You just had a baby, and you're currently nursing," my doctor told me.

"I know it sounds crazy, but I feel life within me," I replied.

They checked me out, gave me a pregnancy test, and sure enough I was right. I was pregnant once again. I went home and told my husband the news. He was bewildered. "It's a girl. I just know it," I told him. "Well, we'll call her Lisa if that's the case." And just like that, as easily as we had conceived her, we had also named her. When I returned from my six-week maternity leave, I had the awkward pleasure to announce I was already pregnant again. At the time, we had seven employees in the department. Five were pregnant and one was a man. People started to wonder if there was something in the water!

I was a little nervous as the nine months flew by, but on April 24, 1989, I gave birth to a perfect little girl. Talk about polar-opposite birthing experiences. With Lisa, I felt no pain during labor or delivery. It was the easiest birth imaginable. Even my medical team was stunned. They never had a mother deliver without an ounce of pain before. For that, I call Lisa *my angel*. I now had even more purpose—two beautiful healthy children—and my heart was full.

As a new mom, I immersed myself in the simple joys of motherhood. The sound of my kids' giggles, the smell of their skin, the way their eyes widened as they observed the world around them, just to name a few. Motherhood became the most fun job I ever had. But I felt like I was doing it alone, and I felt like I needed to do more with my life for the sake of my kids. My husband didn't share the same sentiments as I did on what being a parent was all about. He didn't want to be a full-time parent. He enjoyed weekend parenting instead. Also, his sister was really into parenting and, in an intrusive way, wanted to "mother" my own children. I gave him as many opportunities as I could before the universe was practically screaming at me to get out of this life I had fallen into.

At one point I suggested we start fresh. Dayton Hudson could transfer me to a store in Montana, and we could live in the wilderness. He shared the same kinship with nature as I. Our kids could roam free in fields, and we could press the reset button on our marriage. He vehemently declined. Once his parents got wind that I was leaning toward separation, they, along with his sister, began a custody battle that I will never forget. That was the last straw for me. I knew what I had to do.

It was time to leave. By this time, we weren't even sleeping in the same bed. He slept on the couch, and I was upstairs with the kids. I wanted to go back to school and give my kids a fair shot at a good life. I sat him down and told him it was Montana or divorce. I couldn't make amends anymore. As you can imagine, that didn't quite sit right with him. In his own variation of words, he threatened to end all of our lives if I left him. A shiver ran down my spine as I began to realize I could be in significant danger.

Stunned, I sat on the couch and called my dad. I repeated back what my husband had just told me. Without hesitation, he said,

"Kari, we need to get you an attorney and a good one, at that." He offered to pay for it, and I pledged to pay every cent back.

Fortunately, my husband's threats remained idle. We went to a preliminary hearing in preparation for divorce. We bickered and argued in front of the judge to the point that he joked, "I feel like throwing you two into a ring and seeing who comes out alive." Looking back, I thought that was an incredibly insensitive thing to say to two people trying to end a marriage. In those days, divorce wasn't easy. Then again, is it ever? The judge recommended a home study before we could move forward with the divorce. It would cost us $13,000. We would take tests and be subject to home visits to determine our compatibility and whether or not the divorce could move forward. It was an expensive step to take, but we did it.

The home test was eye-opening. Yes, we were incompatible, and a divorce was an acceptable resolution to our marriage, but we discovered things about ourselves we never knew. For example, I learned I had the emotional maturity of an eleven-year-old. Sure, I was resourceful and smart, I could MacGyver up anything and create things with my hands. But emotionally, down to my core, I was still eleven.

It explained a lot. I was eleven when my mother passed. I never grieved properly or processed her death in a meaningful way. I mourned her death around age fifteen, and it would come in waves. But once I had my kids, I mourned her again. I wanted to know what she would think about her grandkids and the way I was raising them. Since her death, I was always independent and always on the run. I went from job to job, cobbling together a living and looking for the next thing. I matured in other ways, but not within my heart. As it turns out, my husband had an adolescent maturity level as well. We were two kids trying to raise two kids, and it just wasn't going to work out.

I hatched a plan to get myself, John, and Lisa out. Knowing my intentions, my husband fought me for custody three times. His parents hated me. They didn't think I was fit to be a mother. His sister thought she could parent my children better than I could, and thus that family fought like hell to get my kids.

I remember the day of my first court date. I entered the elevator, completely grounded in the moment. *Anything can happen,* I thought. "You have nothing to worry about, Kari," my attorney assured me as the elevator doors closed. But in that moment, I was hit with the blunt-force reality of what the worst-case scenario would look like. *I could lose my kids.* I took a deep breath and thought it through. I knew I was a good mom. I knew I was more financially secure than my husband.

"Wow, I've never been in a situation like this before," I told my lawyer. "I never had to be this responsible in my entire life." He looked me in the eye and listened. I told him how he probably thought I was a loser. He smiled kindly as if to say, *That is not the case.*

"I'm going to win this. I'm going to get a college degree. I'm going to give my two children a better life," I told him. "Mark my words."

I thanked him for believing in me as he finally opened his mouth.

"Kari, you're going to have to bash your husband in there. You have plenty of ammunition. You need to pull out every immature and vile thing he's ever done and use it against him. That's how we win this," he said.

The doors opened, and we walked down the hall to the courtroom.

I had little support compared to him: it was just me and my parents on one side, and my husband and his extended family and friends of about forty on the other side. At least I had my attorney plus two. I spent the next hour doing exactly the opposite of what my attorney instructed me to do. I did not bash my husband. I did not pit myself against him. Instead, I maturely articulated my plans for the future and built a case for all the reasons why I was an excellent caregiver to my children. I focused on me. I told the judge that I would always make space and time for my children to know their grandparents. I would encourage them to play in the grass, eat dirt, run around barefoot in the fields, and of course fertilize their dreams with higher education.

"I've witnessed exemplary maturity today," the judge said in his closing statement. I returned to the elevator victorious and relieved. I won custody, and I could finally take my kids on a new path to what I hoped would be a better life.

Moral of the story: we can move forward in life by knocking other people down, or we can move forward in life by deciding to raise ourselves up.

I think Lady Grandma would be proud.

4

farm life, farm wife

The ultimate goal of farming is not the growing of crops, but the cultivation and perfection of human beings.

—MASANOBU FUKUOKA

Whenever I was feeling mixed up or troubled, I knew I could count on Lady Grandma. She had been a constant source of strength throughout my life. No matter where we moved or what we did, I could always count on her. She was a key reason why I stayed around North Dakota as long as I did.

Lady Grandma always wore a dress and had her hair tied up neatly. She told me once that she had thirteen miscarriages. After losing her thirteenth chance at motherhood, she ended up discovering the Christian Science faith, a religious movement that believed ailments could be corrected through prayer alone. When she carried her next baby to term, she ended up having my dad in her forties and gave up on doctors for good.

Growing up, I remember watching her every morning. She

would sit at the table with a bowl of oatmeal while studying her Bible. She used to tell me, "All you need is a bowl of oatmeal every morning, and you will live to be a hundred." She might have been onto something. She died just short of her one hundredth birthday.

Lady Grandma taught me that you could be a woman and do well for yourself. She ran a business after her husband had a stroke at an early age. I thought it was kind of cool that she was a businesswoman and a wonderful grandma and mother. She was a great role model and really got me thinking about the legacy I might want to leave behind in the world. Maybe I could become a teacher or run a business myself someday. Whatever path I would choose, I knew I and the kids had to leave our current situation.

The death of a marriage isn't easy, especially when your ex-husband's parents continue to fight you for custody despite the fact that you've won each battle. I had to get out of that town if I was going to make something of my life and "do well for myself as a woman." Instead of Montana, the plan I originally pitched to my husband at the time before he threatened me, I decided to stay in North Dakota. As the dust settled from the divorce, I packed the kids up and headed to Minot. Minot is located in the Drift Prairie of northwestern North Dakota. My kids would get to see Lady Grandma and their grandpa more often since my dad and Paulette lived close by.

In North Dakota, I was starting from the bottom once again. I was forced to check into the welfare office and apply for housing and food assistance. I had barely a cent to my name, and feeding two young children made the bills add up. But they depended on me, and I wouldn't let them down. After they evaluated my circumstances, I was approved for assistance. I found a job at a retail store and sought out the cheapest rental I could afford. With a hint of stability returning to my life, I reflected on my original plan: go to college, get a degree, get a good job, and provide for my kids. But there was no way I could afford college. I could barely afford to put food on the table. I watched my son and daughter as they fell asleep in our new home. I had to try, for them. *Maybe this won't stop me,* I thought. I wanted to get my degree before I turned forty.

The next day I drove over to Minot State University. I started with the admissions office. After expressing my interest in enrollment, I launched into my recent life story. "Basically, I don't have money to go to college but I really want to go. Not just for me but for my two children who I just moved out here with. I've made some bad decisions but this decision, I think, is a good one. Are there any grants available?" I concluded.

"We can see what is available that fits your financial needs," the admissions director told me. I returned home wondering what I'd do if I didn't get into college. Could I work my way up to unofficial leadership positions like I did at Dayton Hudson? Could I learn a new trade or marketable skill?

I didn't have to wonder for long. That afternoon, Minot State called me back to tell me some surprising news. "Listen, a few people around here heard about your story. Your tuition has been paid for by a few compassionate benefactors." I did it. I got in and would be able to afford to go. I was going to college!

I called my dad to ask if he and Paulette would be willing to watch the kids one night a week and one weekend day. I explained to them that I was serious about my responsibility as a parent and college was very important to me and my kids' future. Childcare assistance would only be offered if I wasn't working, and I needed to work while going to school. I wanted my kids to see me working, not simply relying on the government's assistance. Knowing this, my dad agreed to the arrangement, and I enrolled in my classes a few weeks later.

I fancied the idea of working as a home economics teacher and decided to follow that path academically. Once again, for someone who grew up hating school, I did really well. I enjoyed what I was learning, and it was nice to be so close to my dad. Having him help me get an attorney for my previous marital situation had begun an unlikely bond between us, and over time he would often call to check in on me. I felt like we were rebuilding our relationship and he was being a true dad to me and an excellent grandfather to my kids.

While I tried to piece my life back together with the ingredients available to me, I slowly started to have hope for the future once more. I had one friend in Minot, a customer I met at Dayton Hudson. One day I called her and asked if she remembered me. She said yes, and we got together to catch up. It was nice to have someone to talk to who wasn't associated with my current work or school. I was content with our friendship until she said, "Kari, I know somebody that you just have to meet!"

I didn't want to "meet" anybody. I had just gotten out of a horrible marriage. I was in poverty, scraping together what I could while I worked on a better me in college. I was in no situation to "meet" anyone or allow someone into my life romantically. "No pressure," she said. "I just think you two would really get along."

To avoid letting her down and quite possibly to maintain our friendship, I agreed to meet this guy. He was a crop adjuster on her farm about twenty miles out of Minot. At first we talked on the phone before meeting in person. I laid my situation out in the open so there would be no surprises. After all, I was just doing a friend a favor. I told him I was a single mom with two kids who was determined to graduate from college. I'm not sure what part of that narrative seemed attractive to him, but the next thing I knew, he came into town with two pheasants he'd shot.

They were beautiful! He cleaned them and said, "You have two little kids, here you go. I take the back roads sometimes when I come to town. I bring my gun so I can get some birds when I see them." I was amazed at his kind gesture. I told him I would love some pheasants, he handed them over, and we agreed to go get coffee soon. Now this is not to say that I'll date the first man who brings me a pair of pheasants. It's just that after me spilling my guts about my life and situation, he still wanted to do something kind for me and my kids. I figured it was at least worth another conversation over a cup of coffee.

After a few in-person talks, he brought me to his farm for the first time. It was breathtaking. There was an older farmhouse and fields as far as the eye could see. The air smelled earthy as the breeze danced around my hair. There was a home-like quality to that farm, and I wasn't even thinking about a long-term future with this man. I just appreciated witnessing nature provide a bounty and the kindness of this stranger as he became a good friend in my life.

The first time I brought the kids to see the farm, I loaded them into a little white four-by-four pickup with an extended cab. We walked around the farm before heading into the old farmhouse. This time there were no pheasants. Instead, this kind man gave my kids white powdered-sugar donuts. By the time they devoured the sweet morsels, a white coating of happiness covered his entire dark-green first floor! We laughed about it. "I've never had this problem before," he joked, referring to his bachelor status. The kids loved having a new place to explore, and I was warming up to the idea of inviting this man into my heart.

I kept finding myself back at that farm and wanting to see him more and more. One day he was combining (harvesting the crop in the field.) I drove up and parked the pickup on a section line. In the country, it looks like a road, but I quickly learned that it isn't a real road. I locked the doors and back window on the pickup and headed toward the combine with the kids. We crawled into the cab and did a few rounds in the field. The kids had a ball. Suddenly, he looked over at me and asked, "Where did you park, Kari?"

"That small road by the field," I said.

He laughed. "That's the section line. You can't park there. What if someone needed to get through or there was an emergency or a fire? You left the keys in the truck, right?"

I paused for a moment and ran my fingers through my hair. "Um, no, I have the keys with me. I locked it."

"You don't lock anything around here," he said, smiling. "If someone needs to move your truck, they need the keys to move it."

"But what if they take it?"

"They will bring it back. Around here, you leave the keys in the car because somebody might need it in an emergency."

I thought about that for a moment. It was not a practice I was familiar with, but his sincerity won me over. From that day on, I didn't park on the section line, and I always left the keys in the truck. It was my first real taste of farm life, a culture that was so different from my own. Two years later, we got married and all moved in together. I finally felt like I had a home. I spruced up the old farmhouse and got the kids adjusted to their new life. I continued to take classes at the college, including some business management classes, and fell in love with my new reality.

Farm life came with some adjustments. For starters, the silence of the land was deafening. I had never lived somewhere that was so quiet before. When my dad called to check on me, since we lived so far from everyone—seventy miles from Minot and twenty miles from the next town—I told him I never knew silence could be so noisy. You could hear the quietness of your breath and the beating of your heart.

The beginning and end of the day was also something that was hard to grasp. I had worked many jobs throughout my life. I was used to eight-hour work shifts. There was always a defined start time and end time. On the farm, it was more of a sunup and sundown kind of schedule. Also, the schedule was dictated by the seasons. If it was raining, you could get a few days off and spend those days catching up on things, bookkeeping, or going into town to pick up supplies. Rain was always a wonderful occasion because we would make time to get together for coffee with our neighbors. Rainy coffee days were one of those simple pleasures I came to love on the farm.

It seemed like the work never ended, though, and you were

never quite in control. You plant the seeds and have faith that it doesn't rain too much because you don't want to get mold or mildew or any other thing your crops can pick up. However, you hope it does rain because you lose everything if there is a drought. My husband was a purist, and I followed suit. He was once accidentally sprayed with Roundup and nearly died. So we used organic fertilizers to keep the soil healthier, which in turn kept the plants healthier to naturally repel the onslaught of pests each summer. We planted based on intensive records he and his father kept. That meant we might plant based on the moon's phase or whatever else we saw happening in nature. It takes a strong person to submit themselves to the whims of nature when livelihood is at stake. But that's what we did, each and every day.

The benefits far outweighed the challenges. I became accepted into the farming community. Me—the odd kid with her unique way of navigating the world—was welcomed with open arms by farm wives. We were our own little tribe. People are very helpful out in the country, and it was a wonderful way of life. For example, when there were prairie fires, we would keep a pickup, trailer, and tank loaded with water in case we got the call to go help someone. We would keep fuel just in case we needed to help somebody. This is something everybody out there did. We even had a local newspaper that was published every week. Instead of breaking news, it chronicled the community members' daily lives, such as "who went where and what they ate, etc." I thought it was the funniest thing.

I also got involved in church life. I grew up Lutheran, but I wasn't really deeply involved in organized religion until I moved to the small farm town. I joined a group of church women, an outlet that would eventually sharpen my leadership skills. I became president simply by raising my hand, and I had to learn how to organize big community feeds every October. The first week of October, we would feed about 450 people a fried chicken dinner, and everything was made from scratch. Our group of about eighteen women would fry the chickens and make the potatoes. We would make homemade bread, pumpkin pie, and apple pie. We had fresh milk, Kool-Aid, and coffee. I loved doing it because I loved cooking, and I was going to school for it. Plus, I had experience from my hotel and restaurant management courses. And my kids, when they got old enough, could help too.

We'd get up early in the morning and have one of the neighbors get the water tank and hook up hoses through the windows to drop them down into basins. The church had no running water, just outhouses and a reputation for the best fried chicken dinner in the county. The ladies and I put an ad in the paper and everybody we knew came out for dinner. It was a freewill offering. Some people would donate some money and we'd meet as a group to decide how to spend the money. Overall we made more money from making it a freewill offering, than if we'd have charged per plate. We'd raise money for those in need and for community projects. I didn't have much experience with group fundraising before farm life began.

I did all sorts of new things. I channeled my inner bead making child and helped make crafts for the kids. We grew little pumpkins on the farm. Once my kids were school age, they would bring a bunch of pumpkins into class for their classmates to creatively decorate.

Over time, I became a master certified gardener. I would teach people about plants and did a lot of companion planting for pest control. My husband gave me the two most virgin acres on the farm to grow my own garden. I planted my own Garden of Eden, and would invite participants over and give them a tour. If people needed help planting bushes or pest control in their shrubs, I was their girl. I learned to get a little more comfortable with speaking and began to put on workshops and training like I used to do at Dayton's. I loved watching that light come on and people would learn, fully present in the moment. I could see them change and grow right before my eyes.

I, too, was changing. For the first time, I found something I really loved doing. I loved educating people, and I loved showing them new ways of looking at things.

Everyone in the farm community was connected to the earth in some way. These people were my people. I felt at home and a oneness as we worked to plant, grow, and harvest our crops. We grew durum wheat, oats, and barley. We tried corn many times, but it never worked out. We also grew canola, flax, even sunflowers a few times. In our spare time, we planted thousands of trees and built shelter belts for wildlife. We'd dig big ditches for water, and it was a beautiful oasis. In many ways, I was nurturing my soul just as much as I was nurturing the Earth.

My husband always wanted to raise kids and took to John and Lisa quickly. He was an old-school dad, but he made sure they learned things and always had what they needed. We didn't really have money, but he provided such a strong moral compass for them. We were poor, but we were happy.

Hoping to make some money to put gas in the vehicles and mildly increase our income, I decided my garden should be put to good use. I planted seeds with the hopes of harvesting some fresh and ripe produce that I could sell to the community for cash. I loved the thought of eating organic produce, and you couldn't buy much of it out where we lived. My dad was a very avid gardener growing up, but we never got the chance to do it together. I remember him saying how much he loved to garden, but apparently I hated it as a kid because it was such hard work. Now it was my passion. I guess it goes to show that nature isn't the only thing that goes through seasons.

I learned to choose the seeds well and harden-off my plants because the weather could be brutal. Between forty-mile-per-hour wind in the summer and forty-degree-below temperatures in the winter, nature definitely proved to be unpredictable. When you walk by, you just have to rustle the plants up with your hands plus let them get really thirsty before each watering. Then when the weather hits, they can then withstand the elements. The plants adapt to their environment. It was fun for me because I grew things out there that people said you could never grow. I had an herb garden, a butterfly garden, two rose gardens, and a small park. I even created a mini-Stonehenge with big rocks we found and hauled over with the tractor. Inside of that was the vegetable garden, our family's sustenance.

I still struggled to adjust to the lack of control we had over the crops due to the weather and seasons. In my search for something more tangible to hold onto, I began to brainstorm additional ways I could make money to help support our farming efforts with cash flow when we needed it most. The produce from the garden was a good start, but I began to explore additional opportunities that would ultimately lead me down a path I never imagined. It was a path paved by a craving for stability and that can be tricky to come by in the midst of a universe that never stands still. Turbulent weather, broken relationships, starting over. The reality is that it can be hard to find solid ground "out there." But then there's Lady Grandma and those mornings filled with oatmeal and reading her Bible. A constant. An anchor. A heartbeat that never changed. And it was seeing those moments that made me realize: maybe it was possible to surrender in the midst of chaos. But maybe that stillness had to come from the inside instead of the outside.

5

produce, potpourri, and profitability

The universe doesn't give you what you ask
for with your thoughts; it gives you what you
demand with your actions.

—Dr. Steve Maraboli

The smell of the soil, the gentle rustling of leaves as the breeze dances between the trees, the satisfying snap as you open a fresh crisp organic peapod. These are just a few of the simplicities I came to cherish as a farm wife. I was connected to the earth in the purest of ways. Planting, nurturing, growing, and harvesting natural elements each day. Every day was its own story. We had a mean cow that would break through the fence and tear after my husband, so he'd roll underneath his work vehicle to get away. One time a pig fell into a pit and many neighbors had to put their heads together to figure out how to get it out without getting killed in the process. Oftentimes it was a lame deer, or neighboring sheep, that got tangled up in barbed wire. From sunup to sundown, there was always life or limb to save.

Meanwhile, I continued to take classes at the college, this time in business management. Unfortunately, my home economics teaching program became defunct. Americans had overwhelmingly turned to convenience items, no longer making things from scratch or doing household budgeting. I still wanted to earn my degree before I turned forty, so I decided business management might be the best route. I ended up taking a class or two at a time. It was difficult but I worked really hard, getting up at four a.m. every day and studying on weekends. I even made the Dean's list, a first for me.

Two weeks before I turned forty I finally graduated with my bachelor's degree. It was a huge accomplishment! I never thought I'd go to a university, let alone graduate from a private leadership university. My kids were proud of me. I was proud of myself. Most importantly, I immersed myself in the fundamentals of business, with a focus on value-driven leadership, which would prove useful in the coming years.

Back on the farm, we lived . . . simply. We always had food, and my kids never wanted for anything. While we shopped for their clothes at secondhand stores, I made sure their needs were continuously met. They didn't know any different. My daughter even started a few new trends with her own style. However, we were always dangerously close to coming up short. As hard as it is to say, we were in poverty. Lower than the poverty level, actually. No matter how much I or my husband worked, we couldn't get ahead. We had all this land but were still at the mercy of the weather or the market and mounting farm debt left behind by the family. Our fate was never in our own hands, and I craved more control.

There has to be a better way, I thought. We couldn't just be stuck in this rat race of barely scraping by. I told my husband I was going to grow vegetables in the garden and sell them at our community farmers market. I was always a pretty healthy eater, but there wasn't a good selection of organic produce in our town. I decided I'd sell organic and earn some cash on the side. My husband didn't particularly like the idea, thinking how it might look. He believed that as long as we had the crops and the land, we'd be fine. But we weren't fine. We were always on pins and needles hoping we could afford to put gas in the tractors or pay bills for the house.

"I don't care if I have to sell vegetables on the street corner," I said. "It is the right thing to do. People need to be healthy, and we need some cash. Who cares if somebody sees me standing there on the corner selling produce like a poor person?" I released my ego a long time ago, and I had nothing to lose, not that I really had much of an ego anyway.

Because once you go out on your own, fall on your face, start a life with someone, realize that person isn't meant to be your partner for life, and find yourself with two children depending on you . . . ego doesn't matter. In fact, I felt selling the produce was as much a public service as it would be potential income. I wanted my kids to learn from me. I wanted them to know they didn't have to sit back and just accept whatever circumstance life put them in. They could do something about it, just like I was about to do.

I had never really gardened before. So I asked my husband for help and read books on the topic. Then I planted my seeds and meticulously cared for my precious produce plants. One by one, tiny green leaves sprouted from the earth, and weeks later a bountiful harvest appeared. I grew things people said I couldn't. I grew large vegetables that could have won prizes for their girth. I sampled the produce myself, and everything tasted fresh and filled with love. Probably because it was. So, along with a few other farm wives, I started a market in the closest town to sell my produce each week. I reinvested my income returns little by little. Even my husband was impressed. We used some of the money for gas because we needed to keep the vehicles moving. We used some to pay the electric bill. We didn't have running water, but we had a well by the milk barn one hundred feet away, a house, and a pump. My husband also worked another job as a crop insurance broker, which provided health-care insurance and helped us make our vehicle payments.

But the farm just wasn't proving to be as profitable as we needed it to be. I had this gut-wrenching feeling of injustice about it all. In this country, when we grow all this food, big processors come and take control of the markets, and the government provides programs that help those who play along with it all. We're at the mercy of not only the natural elements but also the processors, markets, policies, corporations, and neighboring farmers who have a drive to get more land at any cost. A grain tester at the elevator would say, "We're sorry, but your protein is not ideal. You're at an eight instead of a twelve, so we're going to dock ninety cents a bushel." Or if the color wasn't gold enough, we'd face another pay cut. It was disheartening since the processors bleach the grain anyway for safety because rat feces are the same size as wheat kernels. We had no power and no freedom. The lifestyle was amazing, though. We felt so good because we knew we were ultimately the caretakers of the land, including its wildlife and pollinators, and we were feeding the world really healthy food, but it wasn't paying enough to be "nice."

Feeling powerless, I took the vegetables from the corner stand and attempted to sell them to local stores in bulk. It was a pretty labor-intensive job, but I earned a few social skills along the way. I got to know people, just like I did at Dayton's when I sold shoes. I'd go to restaurants and deliver my produce to clients. It didn't take long before they asked me to deliver raw coleslaw mix and gourmet baby vegetables for garnishes. I loved it. Through my deliveries, I found out about a class where I could learn to grow "everlastings"—dried flowers—and sell them. I had saved up some produce money to take the class.

I paid my program fee and joined a group of women on this endeavor. A broker from Montana taught us how the whole process worked. We'd grow them, cut them, dry them, and put them in tall sleeves to ship them off. Then he'd sell them to retail stores and craft stores, giving us a cut of the profit. It seemed like a good deal at the time. Except it wasn't. The guy got all of us to pay him. While we were growing the flowers preparing for our first shipment, he left town, never to be contacted again.

I had invested all this time and money into a venture I hoped would pay off, and now I was left with thousands of sleeves of dried flowers and short-changed by a scammer. The other women held meetings where legal action was discussed. They wanted to sue and get their money back. I thought it was a waste of time.

Besides, I didn't have the money to sue. Neither did they.

"Why don't we repurpose all these flowers we've grown?" I suggested. They scoffed at my idea. "He cheated us; we need to get him to pay us back," they replied.

I wasn't ready to admit defeat. I excused myself from future "legal" conversations and pondered what to do with my surplus of flowers. Then I got a brilliant idea. I could make potpourri out of them. I returned to my fellow downtrodden scam victims and told them about my plan. "I could repurpose them for four dollars a bag as potpourri, if I used wildcrafted filler," I said triumphantly. But they were still holding on to that victim mindset. They couldn't see possibility through the ironclad walls of revenge and justice. "You'll be lucky if you get even one dollar for five sleeves," one lady told me.

"At least it's money," I retorted. "At least I walk away with a profit instead of sitting on tons of flowers while scheming a plan that may never work. That guy is long gone by now." They laughed at me, and I left them once more.

I walked around the farm and scavenged for pine cones. I found other ingredients, dyed them, and made these incredibly beautiful potpourris. They had a nice natural smell instead of a chemical smell. I took them into a local store to see if I could sell them. One brand was called "Badlands Beauty" and included all things made to resemble its namesake. I thought about the tourists who might want to take a piece of the Badlands home with them. I made another called "Prairie Delight," and within a few weeks, stores started selling out of them.

I expanded to other stores until I depleted my flower supply.

This is when I returned to the ladies for a third time. Now I wanted to ask them if I could buy their flowers off of them. They said sure; the flowers were collecting dust anyway. "Thank you, because my potpourri is now in about two hundred stores," I said with a coy smile. A few eyes widened at my revelation, but no one volunteered to join my cause.

I started bringing in some much-needed cash, way more than I earned selling produce. I didn't want to give up on the farmers market, though. I still enjoyed it—the gardening and providing organic options to our community. I continued to sell on the weekends as I learned how to deal with retailers during the week. It took a lot of trial and error. I'd deliver the potpourri to the stores, and we'd ship them out as they kept selling. I made little wood pieces with words of scripture on them. Some would have Christian scripture, and some would have encouraging words like "Love Life" written on them. I would attach pretty organza bows, adding grandeur to the scented gift. Pretty soon, though, the potpourri project expanded beyond my original plans.

On the farm, I noticed that mice kept nesting in our tractor cab. Mice can cause a lot of destruction to the interior of farm equipment. They like to chew on cushions, chew on wires, and do their business any place they like. When you live on a farm, you're going to encounter mice. That is a given. However, I needed a way to keep them out of the tractor cab.

Ultrasonic sound devices needed to be plugged in, so that wouldn't work. I didn't want to douse the cab with chemicals either. I considered putting the potpourri inside, but they looked so nice and elegant, plus some of my pieces simply took up too much room.

I recalled my first time on the farm, when my husband asked me to pull-start an old grain truck. I said "sure" and jumped into the truck cab, gently pulling ahead while the chains tightened on the truck behind me. I'd driven trucks many times in the past when I'd delivered appliances and furniture. The start didn't go so well after a mouse ran up from the floorboard against my leg and ran straight into my crotch. I instinctively grabbed for the small bottle of perfume in my purse and started spraying like it was a can of raid. I saw two mice run out of the opening in the rusted-out floor.

Then I thought, *What if I just used part of the potpourri?*

The pine cone would work best. I could douse it with a strong scent and toss the pine cone into the tractor cab. I remembered my early days at the cosmetics counter at Dayton's. I loved doing the makeovers, but I hated being near the perfume. It always gave me a huge headache. Perhaps if the mice were confined in the tractor cab and introduced to an overpowering scent, their survival instinct would kick in and force them to relocate.

I never wanted to kill them. I just wanted them to go be productive somewhere else that didn't impact my family's productivity or livelihood.

So, I took a pine cone, rubbed some essential oils on it, and tossed it into the cab. It worked! No more mice. So, assuming that other farmers were enduring similar rodent problems in their own tractors, I started placing several scented pine cones in a sleeve and selling them as pest repellent. The more useful and natural products I could put out, the more cash flow I could bring in.

I was happy. I felt alive. My kids were loving life on the farm. My husband wanted me to concentrate my efforts on the farm, but he gave me room to nurture my entrepreneurial spirit. Public recognition started happening after I made the cover of Country Woman magazine, and I became connected to other farm women on a national level. My dad was impressed with my gumption. We weren't rich, but we weren't just getting by, and as it turns out, I liked being a "businesswoman." I had a purpose.

Until one day I went to deliver another batch of potpourri to one of my most loyal retailers, only to find the shelf fully stocked with my products. They typically sold out around this timeframe, and I automatically delivered more. "Sorry, Kari, sales of your products have been slowing down," they said. I was puzzled. My potpourri was a unique, natural, and sensory gift. Maybe it was just the store. I left and went to my next loyal retailer, only to discover the same situation. There on the shelf sat my handcrafted potpourris. What was going on?

"Another product has been in high demand recently," the manager said. "Specialty candles have hit the market."

These candles, in my eyes, were simply petroleum that had been induced with artificial scents. Why would someone want to pay double for a candle that produced scents from chemicals and left your lungs and ceiling black? If you want to smell wildflowers, go and smell wildflowers or dried wildflowers . . . not some waxy artificial substance with a hint of wildflower fragrance.

This was the beginning of the end for this part of my business. One by one, my two hundred stores started to decline my potpourri. The remaining products sat on the shelves as the stores worked feverishly to restock the candles. To say I was bummed is an understatement. I found so much joy and fulfillment in crafting those beautiful scented pieces, and so did the four ladies I had working with me to fill orders. I took the rest of my supply and gave some away as gifts. And from here, it was back to the drawing board.

What was one thing that candles couldn't do? They couldn't eliminate mice! Sure, they could fill a room with a nauseating Bahama breeze essence, but they could not effectively clear mice from a tractor cab. *There is still a business idea here.* I started doing extensive research on pest control. No one in the industry was attacking the pest control issue the way I was considering. Everyone wanted to spread dangerous poisons in the air and murder the mice (and possibly pets, wildlife, and anything else standing in the way). Even if they are pests, mice have purpose. They play a very important role in our ecosystem as a food source for wildlife. You disrupt the balance of nature when you mindlessly kill them.

I was deep in my research when the mice began to make their presence known in more obvious ways. My pine cones were failing, and I needed to figure out why. On top of that, the rodents started getting into more of our things, causing damage, and wreaking havoc. I was growing tomatoes to sell at grocery stores and farmers markets. I converted an old abandoned shed into a makeshift greenhouse. The plants yielded big, healthy, juicy tomatoes that could be harvested in July, which is rare in North Dakota. I had about two thousand tomato plants started and got them to a four-leaf stage, a promising stage for young plants beginning to display their foliage. I nurtured my beautiful little tomato seedlings in a lean-to, making sure they had propane heat in the cold-starting months so they didn't freeze. One morning I went to check on them and saw all the tops were eaten off the stems. A wild mouse.

Maybe a family of wild mice. I knew we were going to make a bunch of money off those plants, and to find them destroyed was devastating. I was pissed.

I left the greenhouse to take a shower and, well, lick my wounds. When I opened my dresser drawer to pull out my underwear, I noticed the mice had chewed through one of my bras. It was shredded! First my plants and now my bras! Now they were stepping over the line! I seethed in my anger and indulged in a brief bout of hopelessness. Every time I tried to make money, something had to come along and knock me down again. I was just trying to do the right thing and do right by my family.

The universe was screaming at me. I had to do something. I was either gonna go crazy, or I needed to start looking at things from a new angle.

When there is something you are complaining about or criticizing and condemning, there is a calling there. There is a calling you need to look at to find purpose. The pesky little mice might just be anointing my purpose. I entertained the thought and resumed vigorous research to determine the best way to get them out of my underwear drawer and away from my precious plants. Still focusing on the senses, I tested various formulas of natural aromas to see what was most effective.

While walking along the farm, I took notice of the trees that died in the winter when rodents gnawed at the bark. But there were also trees that had their bark intact. These trees remained protected in the winter and must have had some sort of scent that kept animals away from the precious bark. I investigated the healthy trees and discovered the sap that drips out from under the bark. It was balsam fir oil, which is sticky and pleasantly scented. I started testing the oil with the rodents, and it worked reliably. I engaged a state university rodent researcher, and he found the same. He said my discovery triggered a "fight or flight" response in rodents, making it a repellent.

This could be big.

I wanted to explore how I could mass-produce this humane repellent and even apply for a patent to protect my idea. Once again my heart ignited with excitement, as it did when I began my potpourri business.

Nature gives you everything you need at the moment you need it the most. And I believe the universe does too. When you're in a state of suffering, reframe how you see it. On the other side, there's some kind of freedom. Sometimes it is the universe screaming at you, making you uncomfortable so you do something about your situation. And that voice you're hearing, be it a quiet whisper or a booming echo: it's called purpose. You should listen to it.

6

when all hail breaks loose

Death is just nature's way of telling
you to slow down.
—DICK SHARPLES

There were so many people milling about. They were shaking
hands and hugging. Occasionally a sharp burst of laughter echoed
among the vaulted ceilings of the large church. A reunion. A party.
In a way, it was both of those things. Gradually the noise grew
softer and softer until it was deafening quiet. It is remarkable how
people know the precise moment to quiet down before something important commences.

"We are gathered here today to remember the life and love
of John Havnvik," the minister said loudly. I glanced over at my
sister, Kim. She kept her eyes fixed on the closed light-blue casket with ornate designs emblazoned on the corners. I rolled my
eyes, subtly so not to draw attention to my attitude. Dad wanted
a simple wooden casket, with geese and grasses etched onto the
sides. He said he was returning to the earth and that would be

best. Instead, Paulette wanted to make sure he was interned in style. She picked out the hideous light-blue creation—the Cadillac of caskets—for my dad to be laid to rest in.

He requested a simple headstone too, but I had a feeling when the time came Paulette would make sure that was as fancy as the blue monstrosity before me. She was all about wealth and status, and pretty caskets with fancy headstones meant money. At the very least, when Kim asked Paulette to close the casket cover prior to the service, she obliged. We knew Dad didn't want all of these people to remember him lying cold and dead. He wanted them to cling to the memories they had of him alive. The very memories that sparked a burst of laughter at a funeral.

Four hundred fifty people showed up that day to pay their respects. Kim and I were regaled with stories of our dad's humor, kindness, and abundant generosity. He used to invite homeless people to stay with him and help them get back on their feet (granted, sometimes they just robbed him blind). He would go to great lengths to make sure his employees and their families were secure and happy. Someone even said my dad helped get braces for her child's crooked teeth. If Dad saw a problem, he'd fix it. He gave money away left and right, always volunteering to be the Good Samaritan for those facing tough times. Kim and I were blown away by the stories.

My children, John and Lisa, sat quietly in the pew. Little John was convinced his grandpa died because he ate worms. My dad used to play in his garden with the kids and occasionally eat a worm just to freak them out. He said people in other countries eat insects, so why couldn't we? He only consumed a handful of worms in his lifetime, but I had to explain to little John, who was seven at the time, that the worms did not kill his grandfather.

Cancer did.

Dad was fifty-two when he was diagnosed with the end of his story. He was healthy his entire life and then got hit with kidney cancer that metastasized into brain cancer in nine short months. He had brain surgery and was put on hospice care in his home. He became paralyzed but still tried to move his fingers every day. He went blind but could always sense our presence in the room. A hospice nurse would come every day and help him with his morphine drip. I remember the day he died like it was yesterday. I had said goodbye to him and told him I loved him before returning home to my kids and husband. I crashed on the couch and fell into a deep sleep.

Suddenly the phone rang, and I just knew. It was Kim. She told me Dad had passed away. I'm convinced my father waited until I got home so that I could have the support of my kids and husband before he left this world.

Even under the best of circumstances, funerals are hard. The dark clothing, the hushed tones, the managing of other people's emotions. This was my second funeral. First, my mom. Now Dad. Just sitting there staring out at his casket made me wish for the day to be over. It made me long to not have to attend another one of these for a really long time.

"I'm so sorry for your loss," someone said to Kim and me as they passed by. I didn't realize that the service was over. I stood up and got ready for the next part: internment. As we exited the church, a gust of frigid North Dakota air smacked us in the face.

A chill ran down my spine, and I clutched my coat a little tighter, glancing down to make sure the kids were okay before making our way to the car.

It was hard losing my dad, but I knew he would always be with me. We were, in a way, emotionally preparing for this loss. But it didn't make it hurt less. I was an orphan now. The grief would come in cycles, sometimes hitting me in the gut and sometimes lingering in my chest. I thought after losing my mother, I was well versed in handling grief. That I knew how to process the pain while continuing to walk through life. Is anyone really, though? Are any of us really meant to compartmentalize what it means to lose a piece of our hearts? I'm not really sure. But I do know that after the funerals, I jumped back into my work, an attempt to reacquaint myself with my purpose once more. Life was continuing to move, and I was planning on moving with it.

And I thought I was handling it all really well. Until one afternoon when little John came over to me and tugged on my sleeve as I sat at our dining room table with papers laid out before me.

"You missed my math meet today, Mom," he said, his seven-year-old eyes wide with disbelief.

"That was today?" I asked in equal disbelief. "I'm so sorry, honey."

To this day I had never missed any kind of school or sporting event he was involved in. I knew it was happening. I just couldn't bring myself to go, to be in public, to sit in a big stadium watching happy kids who still had their fathers and grandfathers. I had so many questions. Where did my dad go after he died? What was he doing? Why did my parents leave me so soon?

And that's when it happened. That's when little John reached into his backpack and pulled out the shiny gold trophy.

"I know that Grandpa is dead, but I'm still alive, Mom."

His words hit me with the full force of a two-by-four to my chest. The air knocked out of me. The heaviness in my lungs. He was right. My son was still alive. And so was I. I had to be there for my kids. They always came first. I couldn't allow my grief to steal what was left of our life.

"I am so sorry I was not there," I told him. "Would you tell me all about it? I want to hear everything."

He happily launched into a play-by-play recap of the meet as I held back tears. These were the moments that mattered the most.

In the weeks after my dad's death, Kim and I joined forces to see what we could do about his estate. Paulette, looking fashionable and well for a newly minted widow, had changed all the locks on the doors to the house and hatched a plan to take over the business. She loved Dad, and we saw a bit of compassion in her before and after the funeral, but now it looked like she was back to her selfish ways. People were crawling out of the woodwork, hoping to secure a piece of Dad's legacy. It was messy.

And amidst the mess, life did go on. I started working on more experiments with my mice repellent idea. I tried different scents and methods of packaging to see what was most effective. When I wasn't doing that, I was tending to my garden and growing flowers for potpourri. The candle business was starting to take over, but it wasn't going to bring me down. I secured a deal with Farm Credit Services by telling them I had a new potpourri that works to keep mice out. We were back in business.

I was also baking fifteen-grain bread and offering these really healthy mini-loaves to our community. I had beautiful flowers and pumpkins I would sell at the local grocery store. Plus, I still knew I was on the verge of a breakthrough with my natural special repellents. With each passing day, it became easier to function and flourish. I carried my dad's spirit with me everywhere I went, hoping he'd never leave my side and somehow help guide my way.

Things started to turn around in my grief-stricken heart.

Until they didn't.

"Kari, wake up," my husband said, his voice slightly frantic. My eyes slowly opened as I focused in on him standing in front of me.

"What's that noise," I asked, stretching slowly.

"This looks really bad," he said, as we looked outside, seeing inches of hail stones covering the ground under the mercury vapor yard light.

I vaguely remembered hearing a thunderstorm roll through, not an uncommon occurrence in North Dakota. I quickly got dressed, checked to see if the kids were still sleeping before joining my husband outside. The door was open as I stepped out to see the worst of it. I couldn't believe my eyes. My mouth hung open as my heart lurched up in my chest.

It wasn't just any storm, though. It was a hailstorm. And at first glance, it was massive and damaging. The crops were flattened. The windows on the barn were broken. The vehicles were all dented. I could hear a pickup truck in the distance, most likely another farmer coming to survey the destruction. A small breeze rustled the nearby trees as I stood with my husband in complete shock and silence.

"The horses? The cattle?" I asked him, unable to form complete sentences in that moment.

"They're safe, inside the barn, but everything is done. This is a total loss," he said. It was something he knew well as his off-farm job was as a crop insurance broker to North Dakota agents. He'd seen it plenty of times but never this bad.

I walked over to my garden to find my beautiful flowers flattened as if a herd of wildebeests came trampling through the night. I kicked several hailstones with the tip of my boot as I continued to survey the damage. I had just signed a contract for twelve hundred bags of potpourri, and now my flowers were destroyed.

Thank God we had hail insurance. Our barn was destroyed. The farm vehicles and roof were going to need significant repair. My tomato plants were eviscerated. There was one small spot in the garden that remained untouched. It was little John's plot. It was overrun with weeds, which somehow protected his plants. The twelve-by-fourteen spot looked like the Garden of Eden. When he woke up, he'd be happy to see that.

But I didn't know what to do. We'd have to clean up and then call the insurance company. I knew my husband would want to drive to the other farms to see how everyone in the community was doing. I decided to go back inside and eat some breakfast. There was nothing I could do at that very moment except process what had happened and make sure the house didn't sustain any damage.

It took days to clean up the garden. My husband handled the farm because he had to figure out what to do since we still had the expense of harvesting the crop even though it was chopped down and worthless at this point. Disappointing doesn't even begin to describe how it felt. We also had to call insurance agents about the crop, vehicles, and house.

With no flowers for the potpourri, I had to make another dreadful call to the farm credit services and let them know my stock of flowers had been destroyed. I decided I would use the hail insurance payout I'd secured on my truck garden to buy flowers from other growers so I could at least fulfill the contract. I had to get the dyes and things I needed to turn them the right color. I needed to feel good about something. In the long run, it wasn't profitable. In fact, I lost money through the obligation. It was a huge kick when we were already down.

Shortly after the hailstorm, my local homemakers club and local church ladies group both disbanded. "Too much to do and not enough time" and "we're getting too old to work this hard" were the reasons given that didn't entirely make sense to me. All of a sudden the groups fell apart. Gone were the meetings. Gone were the expert tours of my garden. Gone were the church socials and days of cooking elaborate meals for the community. My heart hurt and my days became consumed by pockets of free time. In a matter of months, I lost my father, my grandmother, my farm, my garden, and the only social network I had in rural North Dakota. I thought I was so close to having my life figured out, and then these setbacks put me back into my place. It was humbling. I was no stranger to starting from scratch, but this blank canvas of life was filled with deafening uncertainty.

As we planned to rebuild—because that is what you do when Mother Nature ruthlessly knocks you down—I set out to find produce from other avenues that we could sell at the farmers market.

We'd need more income to offset the lack of profitability our farm now produces. Farming is seasonal. If your crops get destroyed, you can't just tear them down and grow the same thing, starting over. You need to plant with the season and follow strict guidelines for the harvest. We'd be able to make ends meet, but a few extra dollars couldn't hurt.

Besides, I loved the farmers market. Since the disbanding of my church ladies, it was really the only other opportunity I had to go out and be social. I loved telling people about my breads or herbs. I headed down to the farmers market that morning. It was a beautiful, sunny day. It had to be about seventy-two degrees and a picture-perfect farmers market kind of day.

The vendors set up tables and tents in an old gas station parking lot from the '50s. The station was now a crafting space with huge garage doors and the lot for farmers markets, craft fairs, or premium parking for town parades. That morning, my table was full of organic strawberries in these green paper baskets I found. I picked up the organic berries from another grower down by the river, so I'd have something that everyone wanted and no one had. That was a key ingredient to a successful market day: supply and demand. If everyone has huge squash and zucchinis, it comes down to price. If you're the only table with gorgeous plump strawberries, it makes for good demand.

I arranged my lettuce, peas, small zucchini, and herbs on the table. It wasn't much, but I hoped the strawberries in large green flats would carry their weight. I also had several mini-loaves of my fifteen-grain bread. The secret is to make it with pumpkin instead of oil and use molasses instead of sugar. I also would throw in a few different types of crushed nuts for extra protein. People couldn't get enough of the bread. On the rare occasion there were leftovers, I'd give them to my kids before they left for school.

The crowd was thick at ten a.m. The big draw so early was Luanne's hothouse-grown hydroponic tomatoes. They were a hot commodity! By 11:10 a.m. the crowd thinned out and we experienced our first real lull of the day. There were about twelve to fifteen people mulling about. I heard kids laughing across the street in the park. I knew they were waiting for my kids to show up, but they were not coming to the market today.

Suddenly I heard the faint sound of a motorcycle coming toward the lot. Vivian, a seventy-two-year old teenager with a long grey ponytail, black leather jacket, and black boots, was out in her Honda touring bike with a sidecar. She didn't want to park in the parking area, so she decided to take a shortcut through a neighboring yard to the market area.

That's weird. I thought. *Why would she drive that big bike on Lila's lawn?* Vivian got closer to our table.

"I don't think she's going to stop!" Luanne said frantically.

Wham!

The bike narrowly missed Luanne and instead hit her table.

Suddenly, a sound came out of me that I had never heard before. It was some kind of scream as I was sandwiched between Luanne's table and my own.

Snap.

The two tables acted like a giant pair of scissors, forcefully snapping my femur bone. I flew backward into the lot from the force of it all and landed on dozens of Luanne's tomatoes as pain shot through my entire body. I lay on the ground, writhing in pain as Lila, the lady who owned the rental space, said, "Kari, are you okay? Kari?" Her face was blue, and she resembled a terrified loon.

"I think my knee is broken," I said between gasps of pain.

Lila called an ambulance as I witnessed a flurry of grey hair and elbows circle around me. Except they weren't concerned about me. They wanted a deal on Luanne's damaged tomatoes that were sprawled around my body! Luanne held my neck gently trying to will away my pain while glaring at the ladies.

"Can't you see someone is hurt here?" Luanne said with disgust. "Move. The ambulance has to get through."

The ladies shuffled away, murmuring to themselves as I started to feel dizzy. I didn't cry. I knew where I was, and I could feel everything except below my knee. It seemed like hours but may have been only five minutes before the emergency team arrived on the scene.

"Jesus Christ, she's split wide open!" an EMT said as he got closer to me. I panicked for a second before realizing he was looking at the red pulpy mess from the tomatoes.

"It's okay. I've landed on tomatoes. That's not my blood," I said to him. He calmed down a bit.

They loaded me into the ambulance. Jim, an EMT with a nearby reiki practice, urged the local physician to send me to the trauma hospital about fifty miles away without stabilizing my broken femur. Thankfully they didn't follow protocol to stabilize my leg. My femoral artery had been pierced by my sharply broken femur. It wasn't my knee.

The next thing I remember was waking up and being blinded

71

by light. I wasn't sure where I was or what had happened.

"Kari, can you hear me?" someone asked me.

I tried to nod, but my head felt like it was floating off my body.

I glanced around and saw nothing but white walls. White. White. White. I looked down. White sheets. I looked up: a white lab coat. The faint smell of bleach tickled my nostrils. Or maybe it was hand sanitizer. I wasn't sure. The fluorescent lights beamed down on me as I tried to figure out where I was.

"What happened? Where am I?" I asked.

"Kari, you're at the hospital right now," the doctor replied, "because you died."

7

from death to life

Everything that slows us down and forces patience, everything that sets us back into the slow circles of nature, is a help. Gardening is an instrument of grace.

—MAY SARTON

What? Am I dead? I thought. But he didn't say I was dead. *He said you "died."* Also, he looked like a doctor. If I was dead, I'm not sure it would be a doctor delivering the news. An angel, maybe. A doctor, not so much. I blinked to try to clear the fog from my eyes. Slowly my senses returned. I felt a numbing pain radiating from my finger where something was tightly clipped on. The smell of Lysol glided through my nostrils. I tried to move, but I couldn't. I was stuck, possibly restrained somehow. I was also very, very thirsty.

My eyes darted back and forth as I tried to recall where I was and how I got there. I spotted a clear plastic bag near the windowsill with my clothes crumpled inside. Before I could inspect further, the doctor flashed a bright light in my eyes. It gave me a bit of a headache. He tucked the flashlight into his jacket, and I blinked the tiny dots away, still trying to get my bearings.

"What happened?" I said, finally managing to find my voice. I couldn't move, but I could still talk. That was a good sign.

"Kari, you had an accident," the doctor said softly.

I thought about that for a moment. *Tomatoes. Motorcycle. Vice.*

"Leg!" I said, as the accident flashed clearly in my memory.

"Yes, your femur was severed, and your femoral artery burst in surgery. You lost so much blood and flat-lined in the operating room. We thought you were gone."

I took a moment to process this, eager for more information.

"Thankfully, your leg was not placed in the required stabilizer at the transferring hospital. One little jostle, and your artery would have blown in transit. Instead, it waited until surgery. Your leg is stabilized, and you're going to have some mobility limitations in the coming months. You are not out of the woods yet. You broke the largest bone in your body. Seventy percent of patients with this kind of injury arrest from a blood clot. Do not try to move your leg. We want to monitor you for a few days, keep you close until you're out of the woods."

I still had my leg! That was great news. All limbs accounted for.

"It was remarkable," the doctor continued without prompting. "You coded and were gone for a long time. There was blood every-where. Eight of us worked frantically to get you enough blood, re-pair your main artery, stabilize your broken bone, resuscitate you, stabilize you. All of the sudden, I see this bright light above all the chaos. It was a very large angel hovering over you. It was fright-ening and I was speechless. You see, I'm an atheist and a medical doctor. I thought I was hallucinating. But there it was, clear as day."

He smiled at me thoughtfully as if he could see into my soul. I blinked back, not sure how to respond to that fascinating revelation. An angel? I wonder if it was my dad, or maybe sent from my dad.

"One thing is for sure, Kari, you are a lucky woman. Femur breaks can be deadly but something, or maybe *someone*, knows you still have work to do in this world. You have a purpose. You are meant to still be here," the doctor told me. "In fact, I'm questioning my own beliefs and will be taking a sabbatical, going back to Germany, within the week."

I nodded. I had a million questions, but I could sense the conversation was nearing an end. The doctor checked my stats and walked to the door. I wanted to know what the angel looked like. Was it male or female? Did it have wings? How long did I die for? I don't remember any of it! When you die, aren't you supposed to see your life flash before your eyes or something?

"Now that you're up, would you like to see a few visitors?" a nurse asked, popping into my room with the stealth of a meerkat. I didn't hear her sneakers on the tile floor.

"Okay," I said, curious to see who called upon me. I wasn't sure what time it was and if Lisa and Little John were waiting to see me or not. I hoped I didn't look too scary for them. But my visitor was a bit unexpected.

"Hey there," she said. I couldn't turn my neck to see who was standing at the door, but I knew that voice so well.

"Hey, Kim," I greeted my sister.

She walked to the side of my bed, surveying the damage for

the first time.

"What the #%?!!, Kari?" she asked me, a smile of relief on her face.

"I don't know. I got hit by a motorcycle and pinned between two farmers market tables and broke my femur."

Kim sat gingerly at the edge of the bed, grabbed my hand, and looked me in the eyes.

"I'm so glad you're okay. You are going to be okay," she said confidently.

"I hope so. I have all my limbs!" I said, half joking.

We spent a few minutes catching each other up on the ongoing things of our lives before Kim, out of the blue, squeezed my hand and looked down at me again.

"I'm so sorry I wasn't here for you."

"Kim, you're here for me right now."

"No, I mean, when we were younger. When Paulette was pitting us against each other and we weren't close," Kim said. "The estate drama, the 'what Dad wants versus what Paulette wants.' All of it. You have always been an independent person, Kari. You never needed anyone. I didn't even try to be needed with you."

It was the first time we really had a heart-to-heart.

"Let's stop the cycle here and now," I said.

"Kari, you're right. We lost Mom. We lost Dad. We don't have to lose each other. I'm here for you. I have your back," Kim told me.

I squeezed her hand and asked her about John and Lisa.

"They're on their way here. Get some rest. You look a little pale, and your hair could use brushing, but overall you don't look too bad."

76

I closed my eyes for a minute and fell back asleep.

What I thought was only a few minutes turned into a few hours. I woke up to a nurse drawing my blood and checking my vitals.

"Oh, you're awake. How are you feeling?" she asked me as she made a few notes in my chart.

"Um ..." I wasn't sure how I was feeling. I felt ... different. I wasn't thinking, I was feeling.

"Honey, you won't believe this, but we had three femur breaks today, all at the same time!" she told me. I would later learn that one patient was a bull rider and the other patient was a motorcycle rider. I was taken first because I was selling organic produce at a farmers market and was hit by a seventy-two-year-old lady on a touring bike with a sidecar. The sheer volume of broken femur patients was enough to bring the local news out to do a story. As the reporter sat at the edge of my bed a few days later, he decided he couldn't go through with the story.

"It just doesn't feel right," the reporter said, somewhat sympathetically.

The nurse wrapped up and walked out of the room. I could still smell that Lysol smell. Granted, it was less pungent than before. I hated that I couldn't really sit up or walk around. I just had to lay there, helpless, waiting for various people to check on me.

My husband came to visit with the kids. They were a little startled to see me in such a state, but after spending some time with me, I convinced them I was okay. Kim came often to check on me, as did a few neighbors and friends of Dad. When you're at a hospital in Minot, North Dakota, news travels fast. You didn't need to make the front page of the paper for half the town to know you were laid up in the hospital bed. I ended up spending three days in the hospital before I could go home, which feels like a surprisingly short amount of time for someone who just died.

My husband gathered my things and signed the papers, allowing me my freedom. It took several nurses to situate me in a large wheelchair that allowed my entire leg to stretch straight out. As they began to wheel me out of my room, my doctor ran up to me, beaming from ear to ear.

"Kari! Kari!" he shouted at a near-inappropriate level for a hospital. "You changed my life."

"Wow," I said, my eyes wide. "You saved my leg."

"I was only doing my job, but you and the angel: it changed everything. I'm going back to my home country to reconcile with my life. I may even quit medicine. I don't know. I have so much to think about, and thanks to you, I'm thinking about everything much differently. You take care."

"Thank you, best of luck to you," I said, smiling. My heart fluttered in my chest. At least one positive thing came out of this senseless accident. Though I was worried that he hadn't forgiven me for telling on him for his bad bedside manner.

Getting me in and out of the truck was an Olympic feat. Getting me into the house was even more entertaining. Our home wasn't handicap-accessible, and I was under strict guidelines to not, under any circumstances, bend or jostle my leg. I wouldn't be able to make it upstairs, so my husband made a bed on the first floor for my recovery. It would be my sanctuary and my prison for the next few weeks. I had never slept on my back before in my entire life. I would have to teach myself how to do it.

More importantly, I would have to teach myself how to slow down. My life had come to a grinding halt. Sure, I was alive, but I was of no use to anyone in this state. I had to heal, and I could reflect. That was it.

"Geez, Kari, you're actually really nice when you're flat on your back," my husband told me days after I returned home.

"What do you mean?" I asked, not sure what direction this conversation was going to take.

"You don't challenge me, and you depend on me more than you ever have," he replied.

"Oh, okay. Yeah, I guess you're right."

I had spent my entire life being independent and self-sufficient. I didn't like asking for help, but in this situation, I knew I needed to in order to survive. In the past, on the rare occasions I would ask for help, I would shut down. Now I practically needed to be fed, bathed, and assisted to the bathroom. Our neighbors offered to pitch in, cooking us meals and helping the kids get to school. I was grateful for the extra help but occasionally wallowed in a mini pity party as I questioned why this happened to me.

I don't ask for much. I selflessly served others. I just wanted to grow my vegetables and sell my potpourri. I lived a humble life. Why did I deserve to lose everything? First, my parents. Then our crops and my garden. Followed by my church ladies. And now my mobility and in a way . . . my freedom.

I sighed, staring up at the ceiling, trying to figure out what I would do next.

Lift your spirit to a higher place. Open your heart to a kinder earth, and destiny will knock.

My eyes widened as I repeated that thought again in my head, slowly reflecting on each word. I wasn't sure where it came from. Perhaps my higher self or my guardian angel was trying to send me a message. I just wasn't sure exactly what that message was yet. It was beautiful. I liked the ring it had to it, but I didn't know what it meant.

The days melded into nights and returned to days again. I felt useless but not discouraged. I surrendered to the fact that this accident happened for a reason. Something good had to come out of it. As I spent more time away from the garden, I began to feel the earth shift my focus. I wasn't meant to plant and grow anymore. The hail took that away, not to teach me a lesson but to steer me in another direction. My husband was already planning the next crop. This was his life, whether he got knocked down by Mother Nature or not. But I wasn't sure that this was *my* life.

I spent a lot of time thinking about my pine cones and mouse repellent. Once we started using them, we noticed a reduction of rodents in the tractor cab. I can't say the same for my tomato plants since they were destroyed in the hailstorm, but my underwear drawer didn't serve as a snack for the tiny mammals these days.

I turned my neck from one side to the other, slowly stretching my good leg. I watched shadows dancing on the ceiling as the midday light slowly turned to dusk. I listened to the joyful laughter of John and Lisa as they returned from school. And I thought a lot about my life. I missed my dad. I missed Lady Grandma. I missed having a finite purpose in this world. I missed growing things and nourishing others. I missed my sister, even though she vowed to stop by as often as she could to check up on me, which wasn't easy considering she had five children at the time and home-schooled half of them.

Sigh. What would I do with the remainder of my recovery time? I had to figure out a task I could complete or a goal to work toward. I could not just lay here, dormant, feeling the vibrations of potential slowly dwindle as my body repaired itself.

Lift your spirit to a higher place. Open your heart to a kinder earth, and destiny will knock.

Gasp. There it was again! That phrase, that mantra, bubbling up to the surface, unprovoked. What did it mean? Was it some sort of code? Was it the sign I was praying for? I said it out loud, sounding out the syllables. *Higher place. Kinder earth. Destiny. Knock.*

Knock. Knock.

Startled, I looked up.

"It's just me," Kim said, walking in with an arm full of groceries. "Got some food for you and the kids. I can only stay for a bit before heading back home."

I felt overwhelming gratitude. My sister really *did* have my back. I listened to the sound of rustling bags as she opened cabinets and the pantry door.

"How are you feeling today?" Kim asked me.

"Less pain than yesterday. Same level of frustration regarding my immobility. I just want to go check on the garden really quick," I replied.

"Kari, you can't. The second you move before you're supposed to, you could jeopardize your healing and progress. Stay put. You're laid up for a reason," she said.

The world kept spinning. People kept living their lives. I felt like mine was on pause. Time was passing, but I felt stuck in the never-ending present, as if I was on a loop.

"Gotta go, I'll see you soon," Kim said, kissing me on the head before heading out the door again.

I must surrender to this loop. There must be some reason my world has grinded to a halt. What is that higher purpose?

I spent my remaining time on my back contemplating this mantra. It popped in my head three more times before I could sit upright and move around again. I started to notice some changes within my body. If a breeze wafted through an open window, I listened to hear its message. When it rained outside, I felt a cleansing happening on my insides. It was as if my accident brought me and the earth together, bound by a synchronicity that I never could have imagined. The earth is so kind. And we must be kind to the earth.

Open your heart to a kinder earth, and destiny will knock.

"That's it!" I shouted to the empty room. "That is it!" Motivation and purpose and excitement warmed the blood coursing through my veins. I knew what was next. I knew what the mantra meant. I'd have to do some research and learn a few new things before bringing it to fruition, but it was starting to make sense.

And with that, the early conception of EarthKind was in the making.

8

taking flight

All human beings have the ability to transform like a caterpillar emerging from its cocoon and taking to the sky.

—JIM ROHN

Lying on my back resembled death. I could see my mom lying on her back in her casket through my childhood eyes all over again. Death. Limitation. I craved freedom and movement. I was losing weight rapidly because my husband was having trouble feeding me. I'd ask him, "Please, make some sandwiches," but he was working so hard, he literally forgot to feed me. Looking back, it is kind of comical today. How can a grown adult forget to feed another grown adult? It was as if I was a child all over again. Thankfully, John and Lisa stepped in and tried to help in any way that they could. My children learned kindness early on, a trait they still practice with gusto today.

Is this how bears feel when they hibernate? Do foxes feel trapped in their dens? Do snails or turtles feel claustrophobic in their shells?

What about caterpillars tucked tightly in a cocoon, unable to move until wings sprout from their body?

As I lay there, my thoughts swirling, I reminisced about the work I did with the church ladies and all the times in my life when I felt called to be a leader instead of a production worker. I fondly recalled my time at Dayton Hudson, when I'd take on informal leadership roles and offer presentations and workshops. I even spent time thinking about the days working at my dad's gas station and running paper routes in the neighborhood. I was happiest when I was outside, and I was happiest when I felt like a leader. As much as I loved being a part of the farming community and working with the land, I had been extracted, quite painfully, from that oasis. From the hailstorm to my accident, I had been placed on the sidelines of the life I loved.

What types of people do I want to be around? What sort of work do I want to do in the world? These are the enormous life questions that I pondered over and over again in my mind. *If I died tomorrow, would anyone remember me?* People surely remembered my dad and all of his selfless acts of kindness. This was evident by the attendance at his funeral. My dad made his mark on this world. I didn't think I had the chance to do that yet. Or maybe I did, but I didn't take advantage of it.

I didn't have an advanced college degree. That was still a big goal of mine. I had diverse experience but not defined expertise.

What is my purpose?

Recovery was painstakingly slow. When I could finally wiggle my toes and shift my weight ever so gently, I knew it was time to work on recovering mobility. I was tired of feeling helpless, and with each day and night spent on my back, I felt a stirring within my soul. We couldn't afford physical therapy, but there was a lady in town that bought my potpourri and happened to be a retired physical therapist. I asked if she'd be willing to teach me a few exercises so that when the time was right I could regain my mobility. Fortunately, she obliged. This kind soul printed out sheets of what I could do and talked me through the exercises for free. Boy, they were tough. I think the first time I tried to bend my knee, it just wouldn't move. My muscles were so weak and my tendons so tight after lying down for so long. My femur may have healed, but my leg still felt broken.

It was agonizing, but very slowly I began to move. I'd wiggle a toe here, flick a foot there, and gently rotate a knee. I couldn't drive. I couldn't walk. I couldn't really work, at least not at first, but I could get off of my back. I was making progress.

Then came a battle I never expected.

After the accident, my insurance company got in touch regarding my medical bills. If you added up the ambulance ride, emergency surgery, hospital admission, medication, food, bandages, and after-care medications, it was ridiculously expensive. I had underinsured motorist and personal injury protection in my own policy just in case I'd ever need it. When paper bills started arriving at the house, it was time to make the call.

"I've received several bills to my residence for services rendered after a woman ran me over with her motor bike," I told my insurance company. "The whole thing was not my fault, and I plan to pursue damages from her insurance."

Turns out, my counterpart wasn't properly insured. Her

insurance company contacted me for a statement and then refused to pay the medical bills.

"You're just a farm wife. There's really no lost or future income to recover here," the insurance agent told me.

I was humiliated. Who even says that? *Just* a farm wife? I had witnesses! Why should my ordeal be worth less because I'm not a leg model? That is what it felt like. As if I was somehow less valuable and not a victim of a freak accident. Maybe senior citizens shouldn't be recklessly circling farmers markets on their motorbikes.

"I have mounting medical costs for an accident that was not my fault," I contested.

"It is what it is," they told me. How professional.

After some research, I discovered I could use their lack of professionalism to my advantage. It was a lengthy process, but in the end, I won punitive damages because of the way my own insurance company treated me when I asked them to pay the claims I had paid premiums to receive. I could sue for loads of money, beyond what I needed to cover the cost of my medical bills, and possibly win. Lord knows we could use the finances. But I didn't have the fight in me. Also, I'm not really keen on lawsuits.

"As long as you pay out my policy limits, I'm fine," I said. Life was too short for a long, drawn-out legal battle. Besides, the lady who hit me didn't have a spare cent to her name. Her husband promised me from my hospital bed to sell the motorcycle and give me the proceeds. That never happened.

My insurance victory was marred by an unsettling feeling nestled deep in my gut; that label "just a farm wife" did not sit well with me. Most farmers in our community had college degrees

and were experts. The farmers I knew were also brilliant nego-
tiators and scientists and community contributors. They knew
the markets. They knew other countries and trade law and what
would prove to be profitable. These farmers were so educated
compared to what the rest of the world thought they were. The
more I thought about that unfairness, the more it bothered me.

It wasn't the first time I had been exposed to labels. Having
always been an "odd" kid who marched to the beat of my own
drum, I was accustomed to being placed in proverbial boxes. Kari
is different. Kari's had a hard life. Kari is a hippie. You name it. But
this time it made me want to prove something. And I had to start
with myself.

Lift your spirit to a higher place. I had nothing left. It had all been
taken away, hailed away, died away. My only option was to start
with what I had, where I was. Bloom where I was planted. Ever
since my accident, I had a profound appreciation for the fragility of
my body. I was made from earth. I felt that more than ever when
I awoke in that hospital bed. While my material possessions were
limited, I had plenty to be thankful for.

First there was John and Lisa, my two wonderful children.
Then there was the hail settlement and the land that was already
primed for new crops. But what about nonmaterial things? What
did Kari have, right at this very moment, with a bum leg and a lot
of big questions?

*I have compassion, wisdom, and the will to make a difference in
the world.* Those were seeds that could be fertilized, and I had everything I needed right at my disposal. My compassion for the planet
was born within me back when I was a five-year-old blond-haired

girl staring out at Kills Dump with my father. The Away made my heart break. Now I was thirty-three, seeing the ugliness in the world again. Labels, poisons, greed. A metamorphosis of human-kind's compassion toward the earth was needed. In my broken-ness, I felt I was being called from within to become the entre-preneurial first responder that nature needed. I had to educate consumers to help change deep-seated behaviors. Once you know the problem you want to solve, you can begin work to cre-ate a better solution than what exists today. My soul craved the opportunity to do something about this need, this role. It was as if I could be that five-year-old girl again, but wiser.

As I slowly moved my body more, like a caterpillar gently ex-tracting its wings from the cocoon, I thought about how I could best care for the earth, care for my spirit, and pay my bills. I had multiple entrepreneurial ventures up until now, but I had never married them into a fully congruent business model. Business has so much to learn from nature. I never understood how peo-ple thought we were not all connected.

My mind returned to insects and bugs. They did not belong in the home, but they did belong in places like the Away. Insects are masters of reduce, reuse, recycle. I wanted to bring this wis-dom of nature to life and one day in business organizations if it all worked out.

Insects. Mice. Pests. They have purpose. They are part of our ecosystem's organizational hierarchy. Perhaps I could develop a way to control the pests without killing them.

Opportunity will knock!

"That's it! That's it!" I yelled out to no one in particular.

I could develop a humane pest control system and turn it into a profitable earth-kind business venture. It was never an industry I grew up wanting to tackle, but it would solve a problem without harming the balance of nature. No more mice in my tomato plants. Solving problems equals money, and I needed money. Heck, maybe the insect kingdom would hear about it and help me next time I die. Maybe they'd usher me into heaven rather than being decomposers of my rotting corpse!

Like the bees we depend on for so many things, I made a resolution to become a pollinator myself. I would begin gathering and redistributing the wisdom I gained by helping people live and work in harmony with nature. I could become a decomposer, breaking down misconceptions about pests, disintegrating the illusion that killing and poisons were the only way to keep pests away. I could share my thirty years of wisdom, educating people about how spiders eat little bugs you don't want in your home and how ants provide termite and stink bug control for the outside perimeter of your home.

Ask the universe for what you seek, and she will provide. These new ideas vibrated through my heart with boundless energy. I felt my purpose coming to light. I even began to appreciate the time I spent flat on my back, pondering life's big questions. Everything led me to where I needed to be. The loss had purpose. The injury had purpose. And now I felt like I had purpose.

We are capable of anything we believe we are. Slowly I became more mobile and could maneuver around the house with ease. My cocoon split wide open as one wing, followed by another, emerged from containment. I saw light. I saw possibility. I had a whole new perspective about life as I knew it and my own life as well. As I leaned into this freedom, I earned more of it. The lady who owned the farmers market lot in town lent me an old golf cart, and with some practice I was able to use it to whip around the farm and do some work on the grounds. Where there is a will, there is a way. Total surrender gives you this gift of will. Once you've lost everything, you realize there is nothing to lose and the reality you had before has died. It is replaced with the truth of a new realization calling for activation.

It took almost losing my leg to realize I was put on this planet to serve and to lead. Everything I needed would be provided to me at the right time and place. I had a heart to serve, a body to serve, and a will to serve. I could lead and nurture the planet at the same time. Destiny never looked so clear and beautiful. But there was a lot of work to be done. For starters, I would have to learn more about the fundamentals of running a business. As soon as I was fully recovered, I planned on enrolling in a business course designed for women.

Women are disregarded as business leaders simply due to preconceived patriarchal connotations from the past. Women can be farmers and make bouquets of flowers, but could they start and run a successful business? We know today that the answer is yes, but back in my day it wasn't deemed plausible. There were so many other things to consider, including my delivery method, materials, the scientific formula I'd need to develop for the product, and patents! Once perfected, I would need to apply for a patent.

I had not felt this excited in a long time. I wasn't selling handmade beaded jewelry anymore. This had the potential to be huge, both in profit and in impact. *Lift your spirit to a higher place. Open your heart to a kinder earth, and destiny will knock.* I finally understood it. It was time to open my heart to a kinder earth. It was time to grow wings.

I don't think people need to experience a life-altering event such as a freak accident and death to reach this point. First, all you have to do is figure out what deeply pains you in this world. What makes your heart hurt? What makes you shake your head in disgust and sadness? Know that it is in that dark place of pain and longing where you will find your will and receive anointing for this work. Your compassion leads you to that dark place. Your wisdom continues to build within you from the day you are born. Your will emerges like a butterfly when these elements align.

9

mice to millions

*Persistence can change failure into
extraordinary achievement.*

—Marv Levy

The fresh snow crunched under my feet as my crutches swung in front of me to gain ground. The cows lowed, sensing my presence as I approached them with a pail of grain in hand. It must have been the clink of metal against metal as the pail clumsily brushed against the gate and held the bucket instead of the closure chain. It was cathartic to be outdoors again, even if it took me twice as long to complete any single task. While my husband was at work, my children and I had to keep up with the cattle and sheep. There was nobody else to do it, and I was glad to be useful once more.

After the cows had their fill, I went to check on the combine stored in the field for the winter. Its work had been done for the season since September, and it wouldn't see the light of day until the spring, but checking in on it had started to become a daily chore. Since there was so much grain to eat, melting snow to drink, and wires to chew, mice would settle in for a winter paradise. Which in turn, would create a nightmare for us farmers.

Mice would come and go, but every nine weeks, there could be a new hatch. All it took was one loving pair, and they would quickly turn into three thousand over that time period. Not even the most durable farming equipment could survive that. Pulling out the combine or other farm equipment only to find that your seats and wires were chewed up, not to mention the stench of mice urine, was not pleasant. Many people would use mothballs to repel the rodents, but they didn't really work that well. And I realized quite a while ago why they'd never actually been proven to work, even if the smell did knock you off your feet. The smell was horrible. On top of that, these moth balls were toxic and permeated the fabric. And so I asked the question, "Why do we keep doing this?"

But as I neared the cab, the scent of balsam and lavender filled my nostrils. Before my accident, I had made the discovery while walking in the woods. I noticed the trees that survived the harsh winters were those with their bark fully intact—the trees that rodents didn't eat. The ones that survived were the trees with sap on their bark. Borrowing a page from nature's book seemed way smarter than what people were currently using. It was now the main ingredient in my repellent.

And it was infinitely better than mouse urine and moth balls!

I peeked in, and just as I had seen in the previous years of tests, the seats and wires remained intact, and not one mouse dared to show itself from the crevice of the engine. It was working!

I was in my third year of testing my little mix of pine cones and oils to see if the mice would appear. Even then, I was my own biggest skeptic. But every time I approached the combine, which was at rest like a bear in hibernation covered in snow, no mice dared to enter. In hopes of giving myself further assurance, I had given it to other farmers—even heading into the local John Deere dealership. I'd toss them a few sachets and say, "Try this in your rattiest combines, see if it works."

There may have been several skeptics along the way, none more passionate than me, but they all agreed to try them. Those mothballs weren't doing much. As I was testing and testing, so was every local farmer I could think of. When it was time to report back to me in the spring, everyone said they had worked.

I was onto something here.

Previously, while still on my back, I had gotten college books from the secondhand store. I may not have been able to afford college at the time, but I could still read and I could still learn. But after seeing that my mouse pouch invention was working, I knew I needed to educate myself further to get a patent, and there were no secondhand books that would teach me that.

But like all things in life, when one door closes, another door opens.

I found out about a North Dakota patent attorney that was holding classes from our local economic development agency. They'd posted a flier in town, so I drove the three hours one way, in a blizzard, to attend the day-long class. I sat in the back partly because the room was packed and partly because I had a feeling I didn't belong here. I wasn't an inventor! Most of the attendees were students from the college or local economic developers.

There were a few inventors: a new twist on barbecue sauce, an innovative knife, a fingerprint scanner. I asked questions. So many questions. After class, I waited in a long line to ask the patent attorney a few more. After all, my drive would be long and frigid, so I might as well gather all the information I could. It would give me something to ponder while the swirling snow would try to bury me. I walked up to the lecture stand, and he glanced up from his notes.

"Yes! You have an idea worth patenting," he said matter-of-factly. "Not another take on barbeque sauce like half the people in here!"

I glanced around to make sure he was indeed talking to me.

"Yes, you." He wasn't overly warm, so I knew he wasn't complimenting me flippantly. "Call my office and I will help you where I can. In the meantime, the library will be your best source for research. I strongly suggest you start there."

I was so excited at the prospect of my invention becoming patented that the drive home felt shorter than the thirty-minute drive to my women's business class. That week I called the patent depository librarian, influencing her with everything in me to recruit a volunteer law student to do the legwork for me, digging up prior art and related patents to erase any doubt of its patentability. There was nothing online for me at the time, and driving the eight hours was out of the question with my kids and chores, so this was my next logical step and it had to work. I wanted my invention to be the first, so finding out if someone else had already gone down this road was important. I would read everything they sent, hours at a time, until my eyes would blur and I needed to walk outside to be with nature again. After going through all the records and finding no prior inventions like mine, I filed the document of discovery—which was free—to get the process going.

I had one year to do the rest.

Normally the time it takes to get a patent is about two to three years. Normally. Mine took three and a half years. It took a while because they rejected it. Twice. "Use" is what they told me, which was just a fancy way of saying that I couldn't invent something that nature had already invented.

"Well, nature didn't put it to use in the manner that I came up with. Did nature mix the ingredients and put them into pouches and place them in tractor cabs?"

"It existed already. You aren't creating something new!"

"But I am taking something that exists and putting it to good use for the betterment of mankind!"

Weeks later, my patent was granted #6,337,081.

I supposed "betterment of mankind" was the phrase that pushed it through.

"I honestly didn't think that would work," my patent attorney said with awe.

"If you keep trying and have faith, things will work out," I said with a smile, holding the letter of acceptance in my hand. I got it!

While we were waiting for the patent approval, we were still making the mouse pouches like crazy. But we needed to name the pouches something. After all, "mouse pouches" didn't have the right ring to it. "Fresh Cab" sounded better. I didn't want to say "rodent repellent," and it did leave the cabs of the combines smelling fresh, so Fresh Cab it was!

I had two employees back then, Lana and Carol. I found out about Carol and Lana from a lady that worked at a local furniture store. In those days we'd been farming without a building to store our tractors, trucks, and tools. With some of the money I received after my father's death, I decided to build a shop on the property. Inside the building I housed my employees, phone, computer, and shipping boxes. It had a water-pipe heated floor, bathroom, and loft for my supplies.

I guess you could say that it housed my dreams.

We took the kitchen cabinets out of my farm kitchen and put them in the shop. It so happened that a neighboring farmhouse had recently renovated their kitchen, so I purchased their 1970s brown wooden cabinets, complete with black iron drawer pulls, for about $1200. I then hired a local carpenter who worked for my father—before Paulette showed him the door—to remodel them for my little farm kitchen. After I repainted them, it was a seriously good upgrade, and I had created extra income for a man jilted by Paulette!

Back in the shop, I then set about repurposing my metal 1930s style cabinets by painting them to a natural light-green color, as the sterile dairy-barn white simply wouldn't do in my new shop. I found other cabinets at secondhand stores and filled them with everything we needed, and bought pallet racking for $800 at a surplus store to store the raw goods and finished product ready for shipment.

Each day I would make my way through the farmyard, the pop of the gravel beneath my steps. The building had two-inch wood blinds with an awning that hung over the porch inviting anyone to come inside. It was welcoming, like most farm porches, and overlooked my two-acre garden. At least everyone who entered felt welcome and wanted to learn the story of Fresh Cab and see what all the hubbub was about. I would turn on the music and lights, check emails for orders until about seven a.m. Then I'd head back in to get my kids ready for school since the bus arrived at about 7:30 a.m. After the flurry of activity, mainly making sure no one forgot their homework, I'd start lunch for my work crew. It would be ready in the slow cooker or bake pan and set to reheat for a noon luncheon with enough left over for dinner. Batching everything I could to save time and money became part of my new life.

The only rule around my table has always been: enjoy, laugh, and love one another. I've found that when you break bread with others, you become community, one with the other. It's the Om, the shalom, in all spiritual philosophies. It's relevant because every link in the food chain is held together by insects and the soil, which is where food begins. Food has always been my connector between soil and soul and the table, our meeting place. Food is so primary to our culture. I swear the only way you can truly know someone is to break bread with them. Lana was a single mom, worked two jobs, held true to her beliefs, and wasn't afraid to tell anyone the truth . . . including the customer. This to me was compassion in action. What I call carefrontation. Half of business is solving problems, and heck, if you can't examine them in the light of day, how can you solve them? Maybe it was her experience as a single mom, or working with individuals with behavior problems, but Lana was a girl who didn't back down. I could have taken three months off back then, and Lana would have everything covered.

Carol was part Native American and a true entrepreneur. She had a part-time business as a root-picker and hired dozens of locals to dig echinacea root, and then she'd broker it to manufacturers for tinctures and pills. Carol had the natural Native American solution to everything, and we'd share our collective wisdom for hours over steaming mugs of soup made from things we'd harvested, which warmed us from the frigid weather.

Both Carol and Lana were good stewards of precious resources—whether that be money, health and well-being, or the environment. My hiring methods back then weren't an exact science. I valued industry and innovation, authenticity, compassion, faith, and moms who wanted to be good role models to their kids.

As Fresh Cab orders would grow, so did my need for hands to package the items. I began hiring the handicapped individuals from Lana's group home, where she worked nights. She was actually the one who suggested that they might love this kind of work. They did, so it was a marriage made in Heaven.

To this day, a percentage of our workforce is handicapable.

But even as momentum began to build, I still ran into roadblocks. I would call pesticide companies to see if they would partner with me. "You're crazy, lady," they would tell me. Well, maybe not to my face, but their answers hit that point. People wanted to kill pests, not naturally repel them. Even when growers were organic or vegan, they still killed pests. That behavior had never been brought to light. No one thought any different.

It was a stretching time for me. My patent application got rejected, my ideas for no-kill pest control were laughed at, and I wanted to manifest change faster than it was happening. There were times where I prayed I would win the lottery so I could expand the business faster and create more jobs, offer more benefits, hire more people. Back then I had more time than money. Today I have more money than time. But looking back, I realize that if my prayers had been answered, if I had won the lottery, it would have derailed the whole thing. If I gained too much—without the wisdom to go alongside it—like a tree without roots, my business would have toppled over in the first storm it encountered.

You see, money and wisdom grow side by side. It's a measure of time and value. The more value one provides, the more money becomes fluid and available. It's a give-first kind of thing for me. I fantasized about what it would be like to *get* first and how I'd give, but it always came back to me taking that first step in faith, blindly trusting that God will align everything in its time and place. Of course, that doesn't keep me from getting lost in the mental commercials of "Wouldn't it be cool if our corporate headquarters had a real waterfall and beehives?"

It's seductive, this human condition. We strive for paradise, when in actuality the paradise we are searching for is all within our reach when we have faith and compassion and see the value in service to our greater purpose.

When I hired Lana and Carol five years earlier, we continued to make potpourri for the Pride of Dakota shows. These were trade shows that invited farmers to sell their products around the state during the holidays. I'd make $3,000 a show and do two to three of them each fall. Real cash. I tried my hand at making candles. However, the cat falling into the bucket of hot wax was the final nail in my soybean wax venture. I couldn't compete with Yankee Candles and never wanted to anyway. Originality in sharing the beauty and utility of nature was too important to me. A triple bottom line of people, planet, and profit was always there when it wasn't being articulated. And selling wax wasn't the way to it.

But as Fresh Cab took off, potpourri went on back burner and orders of the no-kill rodent repellent flew off my table. During one of the Pride of Dakota shows, a news crew came by and, seeing that my booth was busy, decided to interview me.

"So what are you selling today?" the reporter asked as the hum of shoppers echoed in the building.

"Well, I invented a product called Fresh Cab. It'll keep your cab smelling fresh all winter long, and the best part: the mice will stay out too."

That story aired on the news at six p.m. that night. By nine a.m. the next day, there was a line of people two blocks long in twenty-degree weather waiting to purchase Fresh Cab. The farmers needed what I was selling and drove hours to see if what I claimed was true.

Lana, Carol, the kids, and I had to rush home that evening to make more. We had sold out. The exhilaration of people wanting our product—and actually being excited about it—made the rejections of the past dim in comparison. Change was happening! I could feel it! Though our bodies were exhausted, we were finally making it happen, and that was all the fuel we needed to keep us going through the rush. And I was convinced this was the tipping point we had been waiting for.

Early Monday morning the phone rang. I happily rushed to the desk to pick up the call. As I stood in my shop, with the handset to my ear, everything in my body began to change.

The excitement faded.

The exhilaration vanished.

The fuel disappeared.

We came to know them as the pesticide police. That wasn't their formal name, but at the time, I didn't really care. After they heard my claims, they came to my booth, asked a few questions, and left.

"Ma'am, we're calling from the Environmental Protection Agency to notify you that since your product has not been filed with the EPA, you are not permitted to sell this product to the public, nor make any unsubstantiated claims regarding its effectiveness. You have to shut down."

10

regulatory landscape

The only use of an obstacle is to be overcome. All that an obstacle does with brave men is not to frighten them, but to challenge them.

—WOODROW WILSON

The glow of the lamplight reflected off the white rectangles of paper stacked neatly in several piles, inches high, on the small oak table that barely fit in our dining room area. My hair was slightly puffy, a pencil in one hand and a calculator with a paper roll resting on the other. It was the deep of evening so the only sound was the click of my fingers against the calculator, the rolling of paper coming out, and the scrubbing of the lead against the ledger of a long line of numbers. It was my daughter's turn to sleep in the bed in our one-room apartment so I had the space all to myself, which suited me fine. I had bills to go through, budgets to sort out, obstacles to overcome. Funding my fight with the EPA wasn't cheap.

My son, John, had already graduated from Stanley High School in 2006. He moved to Rapid City to attend the South Dakota

School of Mines, where he had received an academic scholarship for mechanical engineering. He delivered pizzas for extra cash and also had some money saved up from his years of growing pumpkins. He ended up investing his cash in Pier One stock, and it split three times! I was so proud that he was making things happen with all of his hard work, not needing a stitch of money from me. My father would have been so proud.

Meanwhile, Lisa and I managed well here in our one-bedroom in Bismarck, despite so much happening over the last three years. Most notably, my husband and I decided to separate.

Before leaving the farm, we lived in the same house for a long time. It was being unfaithful to each other that finally got us in the end. He had his affair, and I had mine. His was his work, and mine was the business. I remembered seeing many farm wives soothing themselves with alcohol and pot and wallowing in unhappiness. It's just a tough life. But I remained sober because I had something to do that was rewarding for me. I played around in nature and figured out how to make some extra cash.

I would help with the farming, and I took care of the cattle and continued to grow the business. As the money came rolling in and the business grew, I knew I had something there. My purpose began to make itself clear, and I wanted to do it full time. I didn't want to do the farm work anymore.

"That's okay," he told me, when I expressed that I wanted to focus solely on Fresh Cab. "I never married you to be a farmhand anyway."

We agreed that he would support me in my business. Instead, he took some of the money from my business account and rented more land for the farm. I ended up hearing about it from a neighbor. Not only had we spent close to three years not being intimate with each other, but we hadn't been intimate with our true feelings either. His friends prodded him to try a little harder. I did my best to support his dream for almost eighteen years. It seemed like a good time for him to support mine. But instead of using my love language, which is quality time, he'd buy me suitcases and travel wear. He believed that working hard *for* me was the best way to support me.

But when Fresh Cab would get some media coverage, the pressure of the business became too much. Between my patent fight and the battle with the EPA, the tension simply began to rise.

"You love the business more than me!" he would say.

"No, it's a business. It has nothing to do with you or me. It's a job."

I could see my numbers had gone down because I wasn't out selling and pushing and living the dream. I was so focused on trying to make him happy, trying to make *us* work. It is a crushing loneliness when you are married to someone and yet they don't share the same passion.

And I think he was pretty lonely too.

We sought counseling from our pastor at church and tried to work through everything as much as we could. Being married eighteen years was nothing to sneeze at. But the moment we realized that we shouldn't be together was a very freeing moment for both of us.

It had been a long day, and he sat on the edge of our bed, his elbows resting on his knees as he ran his hand through his hair. He and I had been discussing the business for days, how it was separate from what he was doing. We talked about being truthful, more to ourselves than each other.

"This is something my soul has to do, which is bigger than anything, really. You can do it with me, or you can do it without me."

He looked down and rubbed his hands together. "Well, you go, girl. It's not in my future to do it with you."

How far was I willing to go with this business?

I sighed and knew that was the final nail in the coffin.

I loved the farm, the garden, the community. But it was time to leave. We decided it wasn't worth it—to fight or lose what little money we had with lawyers. It took about forty-five minutes to write it all out. We chose attorneys and got divorced quite amicably.

As I packed up the Chevy Tahoe for the last time, I stood and surveyed all that he and I had built together over the last eighteen years. My shop stood half empty, all of the contents moved to a different location. The vegetable garden lay off to the side, aching for my hands to work it again. The barn where the cows lowed as if calling me to pitch them in some fresh hay. The land that needed care. Like a seed in good soil, nature had provided everything I needed to grow. Protected by her loving hand, I grew stronger with each passing season and found my purpose walking on these grounds surrounded by everything nature offered. Now it was time for repayment. I had to leave, to continue my quest to expand a new idea, to protect nature itself. After leaving the farm, I moved twenty-five minutes away to Stanley, ND, where I rented an old gas station for the business and bought a small house in town. The garage became our new manufacturing site, while the main building became our offices. The landlord made it nice for us, adding fresh paint, paneling, new ceiling tiles, wiring, bathroom fixtures, and flooring. I purchased light bulbs that mimicked sunlight to replace the flickering fluorescent bulbs reminiscent of a grocery store. It was so worth it. I had a trailer and would haul totes of machined pouches to Minot, ND—fifty-five miles west of Stanley—to a sheltered workshop. There wasn't enough help in Stanley to accommodate the growing demand, so we had many handicapable citizens making the product, and we set them up to do shipping as well.

Within a few years of opening the shop, Lisa and I moved to Bismarck, ND, so Lisa could finish high school in a better school district. Meanwhile, I continued my fight with the EPA. During this time, I would waiver between hope and despair. I would have my little victories only to be pulled down into the depths of defeat when a red stamp with the word "denied" would show up on my applications. But I kept going.

Lift your spirit to a higher place. Open your heart to a kinder earth, and destiny will knock.

I couldn't deny that I felt a strong purpose and connection to prove to the EPA that my claims were real. After all, I was using natural products the Agriculture Department approved of! And few things were quite as much fun as proving the big guys wrong!

Funny thing is, the Agriculture Department was actually the sponsor of the Pride of Dakota show where the undercover EPA officer first did their investigation of Fresh Cab. So obviously the AG department wanted to support farmers that sold value-added ag-based products, all while the EPA was trying to take one of those very same farmers, namely me, and put them out of business.

None of this sat very well with the commissioner, who loved what I was doing and was a farmer himself! Thankfully I had some big supporters in the Department of Agriculture to help cut the red tape the EPA had bound me with, and they wanted a meeting.

I'm not going to lie, though. Initially, I retreated and cried. Balled up with my handmade quilt Lady Grandma made me as a child, I stared out the window on a misty frigid day and mulled over questions, which added to my misery. Pity party for one, please! These were natural products that saved farmers a lot of money, so why did I have to register them? They were made in nature, *by nature.* Why were they trying to shut my business down? And how much more stamina did a person need to have in order to make a positive impact in this world?

Lift your spirit to a higher place. Open your heart to a kinder earth, and destiny will knock.

The saying grew within me like a voice that willed me to go forward. Destiny was always just across the veil. It's a faith walk that I had to meet halfway by lifting my spirit yet keeping my focus on creating a kinder earth. It's like living in both worlds.

And right there at my brown kitchen table, papers piled around me, the fight in me boiled up and over my feelings of fear, and like a North Dakota wind shearing the leaves from a tree, my determination came back. I wanted to know all the details of why they were trying to shut me down. I wanted to look at this realistically, which with my personality helped because I'm wired like that. Give me the facts. Put together the whole complex picture to see if there's actually a path forward.

Four days later, I made the three-hour journey to the state

capitol for my big meeting with key players from the US Department of Agriculture (USDA) and the Federal Insecticide, Fungicide, and Rodenticide Act (FIFRA). The wood-paneled conference room was nearly empty, with the exception of three people and myself.

"It's probably going to be a couple million to fight this," the state employee said with his hands folded and leaning slightly over the table.

"It's extremely unlikely that you will get it through," another added.

"The category for your product doesn't even exist! There aren't even any protocols you can use. It's customary for companies to pay for all of this. Even the biggest of companies have difficulty developing new protocols that challenge convention." The third employee said this with such emphasis that I felt the determination leave my body, puddle on the floor, and quietly exit the room.

"Listen," the first said. "There is no realistic path forward. Save yourself the money, Kari. This fight is impossible."

And just like that, our meeting was over.

I left that morning feeling shorter than I had when I walked in. During the drive home, it was snowing and traffic was slow. I didn't mind. It gave me a chance to take in the blanket of white that settled in the sparse trees, those beings that gave us life, air, food, and, yes, the idea for Fresh Cab. The trees that kept going even though snow, animals, and insects would use them for shelter, food, and a resting place. They persevered through harsh winters and humid summers. Through fires and drought.

Look at your environment. It will give you clues.

If those trees could persevere, so could I.

The AG Department said getting approved was pretty much impossible. In my bones, I knew that they were wrong. I knew that it could be done. And more importantly, I knew that it *had* to be done. The EPA policy hadn't been updated for decades to support the effective, safe no-kill option I had invented. They didn't even allow the words "safe" and "effective" to be used on a label, even with proof. The patent office didn't support them. The regulations didn't support it. How could this be that we couldn't make something that was better, safer, and easier to use and was good for the economy and for farmers?

The next day I called the AG Department and spoke with the head of the pesticide division.

"Here is what I think, Jim," I said, gripping the phone, my heart pounding as if already knowing the fight I was about to endure. "I think this is all bullshit, and I'm going to go forward with this."

"Okay ... well, how far are you willing to go?" he asked with trepidation.

This.

This is where it happened.

Where the question of all questions formed in the air before me and promised to forever steer the direction of my future.

"How far are you willing to go?"

And it's a question that everyone will be asked in some form or another throughout the course of their lives. Maybe not in so many words, and maybe not with such direct intention. But there will come a time. A time when you are asked to choose between your purpose and everything else.

I paused, feeling the electricity fill my veins as the answer came to me without hesitation: "Until I can't go any more."

And I meant it. I had been uncovering my purpose throughout most of my life. As a child. As an activist. As a lover of this world we share. I had articulated my purpose while I was lying on my back with nothing but time left to pull away the layers. And I was being asked to become one with that purpose, to let it shape me and motivate me and become the backbone of the decisions that would stand before me.

"Until I can't go anymore."

I asked what seemed like the next logical question: "Now what do I do next?"

He referred me to Karen Pither, a consultant out of Missouri who was a smart no-nonsense woman. She was a good person and incidentally grew up on a farm. When I called her with all of my information, she told me, "I'll help you. I think this is a really good idea and, hey, I think it would be fun to show the government something." She clearly wasn't willing to take any BS from anyone, and I immediately liked her.

I did as much legwork as I could to save costs, and Karen helped me determine what I could and couldn't do. She had worked for one of the largest global companies in global regulatory affairs, so she knew the ropes and the politics and could see around corners.

The first step was that the EPA had to approve the testing protocol, which was very difficult to decide on since nothing existed already to test no-kill rodent repellents. Nothing. The only guide any of us had was for poisons or traps, which counted dead bodies.

And counting dead bodies was easy.

The problem was we weren't killing anything. Instead, we were repelling.

So we had to prove that our natural products worked in a natural environment.

"You need to prove to us that this actually works in nature. Set up a testing site to prove to us that this repels them in a natural environment."

First of all, how could we mimic nature in a test? It gets cold, a mom mouse moves inside near water, food, nesting materials, and wires for gnawing. We came as close as we could to merge what the scientists at the EPA wanted to see versus the way the product was used. They had to match. Since it was used in storing farm equipment, we found four-by-eight-feet aluminum tanks. We put tubing in between two of them. We then put the product on one side and put food and water on both sides. We'd then track the tank preference. We measured food eaten and droppings and even set up a trip wire to track activity. It was a lot of counting since wild house mice can run in for food up to twenty times a day, eating some, caching some. In and out, in and out. We needed to know what percentage of time they'd stay out of the treated area.

We ran the tests for thirty days and did about eight replicates. We had to hire an animal welfare committee, ensuring the mice were individually wild-trapped, fed properly, and let back into the wild when the lab studies were done.

In a nutshell, monitoring mouse poop wasn't the highlight of my day.

We had mixed results at first because we had hierarchical behavior happening. We put too many mice in the environment at once, and they started tearing each other limb from limb to compete for the females and the "repellent-free" tank. The smaller rodents were forced into the treated side. They'd enter a few inches, hide next to the entrance until the bigger rodent moved back to his preferred scent-free corner, then come back out.

It was time to rethink things.

We added more tanks and split up the mice to get behavior that was aligned with how they would behave in the wild. But the EPA didn't accept it. We repeated again. Still not accepted.

Each time I would think to myself, "This is unreal!" yet something inside kept me going. I knew the product worked and the science was good. I just had to prove it.

Meanwhile, as we were testing, our state allowed me to sell Fresh Cab within North Dakota. They weren't going to arrest us or issue fines or anything because they all used the product, they knew what it was made from, and they knew that the EPA fight was unnecessary.

"You can sell it, during this fight, but you can't go outside the state lines because we can't control anything that happens there."

I just couldn't make overt claims that it was a rodent repellent, so I advertised *The Fresh Way to Keep Mice at Bay*. It worked for the short run, and I didn't *exactly* say "repellent."

But that didn't stop others from accusing me of being a snake oil salesman. There was no scientific proof behind my claims. Yet. But those that had their hands in poisons still looked at me like I was crazy. People would continuously ask me, "How far are you willing to go with this?" Their excuse would be "At least you can still sell your products in the state of North Dakota." Even Canada was purchasing my products. If I really wanted to, I could avoid the fight with the EPA altogether and still be in business.

But again, I'd be faced with the question, "How far are you willing to go?"

I couldn't shake the feeling that I must keep going. I had to prove that this was scientifically valid. And I wanted to play by the rules. To be legitimate in every way possible. I wanted to show that there was a better way to take care of a rodent problem other than killing. The status quo was not healthy for people, planet, or entrepreneurship, and I knew it. It simply made no sense that 98 percent of all products sold to control rodents were toxic, and the other 2 percent were made up of inhumane sticky pads or ultrasonic devices that would drive my pets nuts.

But even in the midst of the storm threatening to break apart the company I had built, there were the little wins that kept me going.

Every farmer who thanked me for my invention was a win. They'd say they swear a lot less now. *That was kind*, I'd think. They'd say they lost a farm dog once to rat poison but never again with my invention. *That was kind*, I would think. They'd say it smelled better than mothballs. That was kind too.

But like the other side of the coin, there was the other side of opinion.

Rejection.

Denied.

No science backing your claims.

Snake oil salesman.

Divorce.

This was all a lot to take over such a short period of time. But as Friedrich Nietzsche wrote in *Twilight of the Idols*, those who have a *"why* of life . . . can put up with almost any *how."* And while my life may not have been on the line in all of this, my purpose was, and that was all I needed to endure the onslaught of what life was throwing at me.

I made the conscious decision to take all of that pain and transform it into kindness. The more people and farms I knew I'd helped, the more my spirit was lifted. I began to understand what the pain and suffering discussed in my theology class was all about. I saw pain as a portal to self-transformation and eventually market transformation. Being pissed off about the mice helped me take action. But feeling like my work was making peoples' lives a little easier kept me going.

As we continued with our testing for the EPA and we would continuously see the same results—that my invention did indeed work—that was a win as well. I saw proof that my science was valid.

And eventually, on a beautiful day in April, so did the EPA.

11

twin flames

*What greater thing is there for two human souls,
than to feel that they are joined for life—to
strengthen each other [and] to be at one with
each other in silent unspeakable memories...*

—GEORGE ELIOT

The condensation of the beer dripped in circles onto the sturdiest wooden and slate table in town. I had been invited to a Thursday night "beer" ritual at Harry's Tavern with a man named Jim, whom I had met months earlier in a sort of serendipitous meeting. He was a kind man, all six feet four inches of him, and I felt safe around him.

We were there with Scott, a sales leader at Jim's same company, Ryt-way. He and Scott worked out all the issues of the company on a bar napkin each Thursday night. They both liked beer, and it felt good to laugh with them all.

Tonight, Scott's girlfriend joined us so it was an even four.

I wiped up the water that was now pooling around my mug

and took a sip as the men continued their banter.

"I say we could, if we set up a new line over here," Scott said triumphantly.

Jim rested his elbow on the lacquered tabletop and quietly mulled over Scott's solution.

"Let's try it!"

I smiled knowing Jim and his quiet way of decision-making. He gave those he trusted room to make decisions, but if you take too long, he will say, "Let's make a decision or dead people will start falling from the sky." (Jim used to be an air traffic controller.)

Suddenly my phone rang, interrupting Jim and Scott's banter. I looked down and quickly answered.

"Hello?"

"Kari? This is Karen."

My eyes grew wide and I looked at Jim, who stared at me intently trying to figure out what was going on. Apparently, so did the other two because the only thing that could be heard was the din of others' conversation and the tinkling of glass from the barkeep stocking the shelves.

I hung up my phone and looked at everyone with a triumphant smile. "We did it! We won. The EPA has just approved our registration."

A great cheer reverberated through my bones as the others celebrated too, having no idea how big it really was. As we gathered around this high-top table, we shared small hugs and larger ones as I felt the wave of relief wash over me.

"One lava cake please!" Jim shouted through our hugs and congratulations and my tears. The waiter nodded with a smile and hurried to the back, used to Jim's jovial voice. I noticed the way

Jim's skin wrinkled at the edges of his eyes as he looked into mine and beamed. I couldn't believe it. The EPA had agreed, and now I got to share the moment with this man with whom my heart had become so connected, at our little high-top table. A table not unlike the one where we first met.

Being holed up in the back corner of the airport bar surrounded by men was not what I had intended when I signed up to get on a plane to Chicago that day. I was headed there for the Pack Expo to purchase packaging equipment for EarthKind. But instead, here I was, the plane having mechanical issues, so everyone decided to do the next best thing while they waited. Go to the bar.

I glanced down at the dark wood of my table and sipped iced tea, feeling like all eyes were on me. Maybe it was because I was the only female in the bar. Most likely they were all going to the Pack Expo as well, and not many women attended. Here I was breaking the status quo again, even in a little airport bar.

"Uh, do you . . . do you mind if I take this seat?"

I lifted my head and saw a man that could have been easily twice my height standing behind the only free spot left in the bar. He looked as if he was a cross between a boy scout and a cop, with blue eyes, blond hair, and a mustache.

"I'll buy you a beer for the privilege to sit down with you," he said with a smile.

"No thanks, I've already got an iced tea, but suit yourself, have a seat." I waved to the open chair across from me in a nonchalant manner.

There wasn't much talk. I kind of felt like he was in my space, but there were no other seats, and what was I going to do: say no and leave it for no one? He sat down and we didn't talk too much. He just did his thing and I mine.

Moments later, the entire place got back on the plane, and two seats away from me was the same man. His six foot four, 230-pound frame, snug in the tiny seat.

"You look like a bird crunched up in that seat," I said, laughing.

He blushed and laughed it off.

"Here, you can use this seat too." I motioned to the seat next to us. "You might want to get an aisle seat next time."

"I'll keep that in mind," he remarked with a warm smile.

I adjusted my white silk kerchief, tied in a neat knot at the front of my neck, and moved my black suede duster coat over my knees for warmth. I was still pretty western back in those days. I glanced down and began to read as he reached in his pack to get his laptop for work. Both of us just a seat away, not knowing that this would become a recurring theme for the weekend.

In the shuttle on the way to the hotel, I happened to look up, and there he was, seated across from me on the packed bus. Our eyes met and he smiled. As the bus hissed to a stop, we both got out at the same hotel.

What is going on? He is everywhere I am!

I didn't feel bristled. If anything, I felt the opposite. Especially when he held out his arm for me to go first to the check-in counter. Finding a gentleman to give up his turn is rare.

"Yes, so you have to cross the skyway to get to your hotel," the concierge told me. "Through those doors and to your right."

I nodded and headed through the glass doors, leading to the tunnel, which bridged the gap between the hotel towers. As I kept a quick pace, I noticed someone walking beside me. Or rather, more like towering beside me.

"Oh, are you over here too?" I asked, getting used to the idea that I was going to see this guy for the rest of my day.

"Yeah, I guess I am. I didn't know which desk to come to," he responded with a kind smile. The wrinkles at the corners of his eyes told me he smiled more often than not.

"Okay, let's walk over together, then. I think it's through here."

As we kept pace with each other, my thoughts slowly drifted from my mental checklist to the strange fact that this very tall man seemed to be my traveling companion today. It was surreal how often we kept bumping into each other. But again, this wouldn't be the last. I would see him on the elevator every morning when I went to the Pack Expo and every evening when I returned to the hotel. There were seven elevators at our disposal, and yet he ended up in mine every time!

The next evening I was invited to dinner by a family that I had just met. And sure enough, sitting there at the table was the man, looking just as surprised as I was.

"Did you ever see the movie *Serendipity*?" he half joked. "Because this is starting to feel very similar."

"I don't have time to watch movies," I answered.

He laughed and pulled out the chair for me to sit.

"My name is Jim," he said as I sat down.

"Kari," I replied with a smile.

Jim was a good questioner. He didn't talk much but enjoyed learning about other people. By the end of the evening, he had learned where I was from, and I had learned all about his teenage daughters, whom everyone could tell he adored. My friendship with him grew a little that evening as the familiarity of our lives edged closer to each other.

"Come on, doofus! You forgot your shopping bags!" I called after him with a laugh as dinner ended and he rose from the table, leaving all his shopping bags he had bought for his daughters.

He looked flushed. "Oh, I . . . yeah. Thanks." He scooped them up, flashed a smile, and then walked away.

The next day I was pretty much finished with all that I had seen at the Expo. I didn't find the equipment I needed, but got names and numbers, then decided, *What the heck, I'll go to the spa.* I hadn't done anything like that before, so I decided to book a facial and a deep hair conditioning.

As I sat there under all the creams and the scent of aromas I'd never smelled before, I began to think about this trip to Chicago. I was scared and overwhelmed at first. My ex-husband and I still had a good relationship, and the one thing he was always willing to help me with was the equipment part of EarthKind. I didn't know much about the machines that we worked with, and he was usually the person to fix stuff if it broke down. Even after we were divorced, he'd come in once a weekend and see if there was anything that I needed help with on the equipment.

But he wasn't there this weekend. And I was just fine.

That day I made the conscious decision that I would never need to ask my ex-husband for help with anything ever again. I could do this. It's the one thing entrepreneurs ask themselves: "Are they capable of doing the things that need to be done for their business?" And I think people who go through divorces ask themselves that too: "Can I do this?"

That day I told myself I could. I could do all of it. And I would be incredibly happy. I would remain single and be a great grandmother. I would be an entrepreneur, changing the way people looked at pest control. I would go to these packaging expos if I had to and learn about the machinery that I needed. I was fully capable, and I would be 100 percent okay with all of this.

The moment I let go of all preconceived notions of how my life *should* have been, I felt lighter, happier, more joyful. I came back from the spa feeling great, and I decided to stop in the bar for a beer. I had ended earlier than everyone else, the bar was empty, and I needed to celebrate my newfound courage.

I sat at a tabletop next to an empty chair and looked around. No one was there and the only noise was the drone of football.

"What would you like?" the waiter asked.

"I'll take a beer, please," I said.

"Small or large?"

Feeling very confident, I answered with a smirky smile, "Today, I'll take a large."

He nodded and left to fill my order.

I had to cherish this new life. I am going to take care of myself from now on, maybe even have a spa day once a month. After all, I could do this.

My beer showed up, and the glass was about a foot and a half high.

"You've got to be kidding me," I said, laughing.

"Well you ordered a large," the waiter said, grinning as he left my bill.

Just then the convention let out. In streamed hundreds of men within minutes, and here I was at a table by myself, only now instead of iced tea as I had at the airport, I had a foot-and-a-half-tall beer with an empty chair next to me.

Oh my God, they are going to think I'm a hooker.

Once this absurd realization hit me, I began to look around frantically. What should I do? I was not going to leave this beer. I needed to get my money's worth. Was there somebody that I knew—

Cue stage left, where in walked Jim. I flagged him down and he approached with an amused smile on his face.

"Wow! You're my kind of girl, you really enjoy beer," he said, looking at the large glass on the table.

"Well, normally I am not, but I just happened to order the biggest one in the house, and now I'm sitting here, all by myself drinking this huge beer, and people are going to think I am a hooker!"

Jim let out a roar of laughter as I continued. "Jim, listen. Will you sit down with me so I can avoid anyone making an offer on me?"

"Of course, I'd love to have a beer," he smiled.

"You can have mine!" I slid the giant cylinder to him.

"No, I'll get my own," he replied with an amused smile.

All afternoon and evening we talked about everything under the sun. We talked about politics, religion, and everything that was wrong with the world and everything that was right with it too. It was like I had found a lost part of myself because we thought and felt so much of the same things. And that was so grounding and comforting.

Years later, he tells me I was more of an extraordinary human rather than his future spouse. And I wasn't thinking of anything like that when I first met him either. I had just surrendered my mind and soul to be happy with the life I was given. I had learned to love my single self and all that came with it. It wasn't even remotely in my periphery that I even wanted to meet a guy.

Jim had missed box seats to the Bears game that night, so he could stay and continue our conversation. He was enjoying himself so much. We exchanged cards and committed to staying in touch.

As the dregs of the beer were gone, and the place was closing, Jim stood up with a quizzical look on his face. "You know, you are the most fascinating person. I don't think I've ever met anybody so positive in my life, and you're knowledgeable. I just . . . that is really incredible."

I smiled as I gathered my things and said, "You, too, Jim. You really are the kindest man I have ever met."

We both went to our separate rooms afterward, and I lay awake almost all night. I couldn't sleep, I felt something come alive in me. There was this new energy. As though a missing piece of myself was found.

The next day I had to navigate a new flight plan, which was switched out of O'Hare Airport to Midway Airport, on the south side of Chicago. It wasn't a huge deal, but it meant catching a cab and driving to another airport a few miles away. As I fumbled with my coat, I stepped onto the walking runway. And sure enough, coming in the opposite direction was Jim. Both of our mouths dropped open.

"I'll come around to you," he called, and I nodded, my heart pounding.

He came back around and set his case down as he ran his hand through his hair.

"This is really strange," I said, glancing around.

"I know, this is really weird," he agreed. It looked as if he wanted to say more but couldn't form the words.

"There's something here we can't ignore. I don't know what it is."

For the first time, Jim put his arm around me. Even though there was a space between us, an energy came through. It was indescribable. We were standing almost two feet away, but it was as if fire circled the two of us.

It scared the shit out of me.

"Did you see that?" I asked, as I took a step back quickly.

"Wow, that was really powerful," he said, equally shocked.

"I . . . I have to go now," I said as I moved away from him quickly.

I didn't hear from him, but I couldn't stop thinking about him. What in the world was that? What happened between us? It was something otherworldly, but I just couldn't ignore the fact that we were two strangers weeks ago, and yet when we were together, it was as if we were whole.

Somebody once told me, "You two are twin flames." Which I later googled. Twin flames are separate pieces of a person's soul— their energies split amongst the two—who do their journey and then come back together to finish up. That totally made sense to me because it described so many of the things that happened. I felt whole with him.

Ten days later I called him. "I'm still thinking about you. I can't get you off my mind."

"Me too," he answered.

"I don't know if this is about equipment or if we're supposed to work together, but something is keeping us connected. I really feel that we need to talk."

Over thousands of hours of conversation, I opened myself back up to a human who shared a similar soul. He was so present with me. He supported me, challenged me, and allowed me to grow into the purpose that I am called to. He is my twin flame, and I feel so whole with him, which helps me feel whole enough to continue the fight for the environment.

All entrepreneurs need an entire ecosystem of support. Like the periodic table of elements, which contain the building blocks of life, having people in your life who believe in you is an important part of an entrepreneur's ecosystem of support—whether they know it or not.

In my case, Jim Block was an element that woke me up to a side of myself I didn't know I had, and later he became a building block in EarthKind with his ability and experience in architecting systems.

I'm the scientist, and he's the mathematician. The creative and the logical. Together, no vision is too big, and no detail is too small. Plus, he doesn't naturally challenge things. I do.

I sense things, even when no one can see them. He has to see them to believe them. Maybe that's why I never liked math and always loved science. Both have an order to them.

My joy comes when in the midst of my work I can help others find or see their own purpose. Jim says our only purpose is to be who we are. Yeah, he's smarter than me. He is the "I am" and the "Om" embodied. I haven't fully got there yet. I try every day.

Being a changemaker means creating harmony where there is disharmony. And that can cause suffering without someone by your side that will emotionally support you. Every day Jim tells me how he's amazed with me at creating change in a way that doesn't create polarity but rather creates a common ground. And he reminds me, in my quest for this business and all that it stands for, that he's the one thing I will never have to worry about. That enables me to fight from a place of wholeness and bring that wholeness to our environment.

Little did I know I would need every ounce of this wholeness when I suddenly had to choose between the person I wanted to be and the business I wanted to grow.

12

integrity

*If you are working on something that
you really care about, you don't have to
be pushed. The vision pulls you.*

—STEVE JOBS

The binders hit the table with a slap as I sat down with a sigh. "Alright, Barbie, where did we leave off?"

Barbie couldn't have been taller than five feet four inches, but her command of a room made her seem much taller.

"Okay, you have got to figure out the extra margin because they are going to reject a pallet here and there. That is just what they do."

I mulled that over as I scribbled on my pad of paper. Walmart was a huge step for EarthKind, but I had wanted more visibility, and that big-box store was another step at success. Or so I thought.

Months earlier, after filling my belly with molten chocolate surrounded by a fluffy cake in celebration for our EPA approval, I had to get back to work. Immediately, I notified a couple of merchants that had been waiting in the wings to begin national sales. John Deere was one of those companies. They had been faithfully selling Fresh Cab in their North Dakota stores and were looking to continue with other states. Tractor Supply Company was the other.

Walmart was the next big fish that we had our eye on, and I hired a consultant to help me put together a proposal for the merchant at Walmart. Originally, I had heard from my inventors class that Walmart was actively looking for new innovations. The program was called WIN, Walmart Innovation Network, and for thirty-five dollars, they'd assess the marketability of your invention. Questions such as "Is this good for humanity?" and "Does it improve quality of life?" were part of the assessment. Walmart was way ahead of the game back then in looking for social and environmental innovations. But as far as the ability to mass-produce it, my score was really low because we weren't automated. At the time, we were still making most of it all by hand. Upon their assessment, they said Fresh Cab wasn't good enough to make it on the market. My marginal score actually gave me hope, seeing such high scores in areas other than manufacturing.

But I had a purpose, and part of that was to bring awareness and a choice of pest control to a market that was set in its ways, no matter how nonautomated we were.

I reached out to Walmart, and then I worked my way from there to find the right merchants, the people who actually bought products to sell in Walmart. These merchants were like CEOs of their category, and I planned to go right to the top.

But I needed help.

I had heard that there was a specific way to present packages to them. Price points were a necessity, and I wasn't aware of the lingo being used within the industry. That's why I hired Barbie, whom I figured was a worthy investment even though I didn't have much to spare.

Barbie was a girl who once worked at Walmart. She lived in Bentonville and used to be one of their merchants. "Show me how they rate success," I told her. If the assessment said that Fresh Cab wasn't good enough to make it on the market, I was going to prove them wrong by showing them that it would be commercially viable.

Profit matters more than anything in the business, and Walmart not only had the lowest price, but they had the highest margin requirements I'd ever seen, and every cost of doing business with them needed to be considered before I made a proposal. Walmart was famous for putting companies out of business that didn't understand this. They certainly weren't known for being upfront like other retailers I was used to working with, most of whom wanted a mutually profitable relationship so they could build brand loyalty together.

Before I went in, I had all of this stuff already planned out. I knew which product would go into each category, the size pack it would need, and the price point at which to sell. And I had to do this at my own absolute lowest price point. There were no negotiations with Walmart.

After months of preparing, I had a meeting set with the merchant. I was nervous, of course. I'd put $10,000 into consulting to save a bad mistake that could cost the business. I'd tell myself, "You gotta spend money to make money." With the flights, rooms, and time I'd put in to prepare for my meeting with this person, it all added up and I needed to nail it.

I found myself thinking about Sam Walton, the founder of Walmart, who originally installed signs above the door that said, "Made in America." The day after Walton died, in 1992, his kids immediately replaced them with signs that said, "Lowest prices, guaranteed." My dad loved Sam Walton and even bought the stock when it first came out. What I didn't know at the time was that publicly held retailers buy stock in products they sell, so disrupting another publicly held company in the same category was next to impossible. It gives them a cozy level of protection and keeps the small business innovations out of the market, even when they are in the best interest of the consumers and planet. There had been no disruption in the category until EarthKind came on the scene.

The conference room at headquarters looked like it belonged in North Dakota. There were no luxurious chairs and mahogany conference tables. As a matter of fact, it was very plain and functional. The room had a rectangular grey table, black plastic chairs efficiently tucked in, and folding doors to split the room in two if needed.

The buyer I met with was warm and kind. He loved my product and immediately took it up the chain, resulting in a few purchase orders within the next four months. This was record timing. Usually it's an eighteen-month process, so I'd hit the line review timing perfectly.

People would say, "When you get the call from Walmart, it's the best day of your life and it's also the worst day of your life."

They kind of go together when there's that much scale involved.

I heard good stories like "Walmart is our most profitable customer; you just have to get the pricing right." I made sure of this, kept an open mind, and met all their partner requirements. I believed the "Made in America" campaign. Turns out, it was putting lipstick on a pig. It's still a pig. I now know we were too small, too fragile in our growth, to even give it a try.

"You've got to be kidding me." My hand shook as I read the first few purchase orders that came in from Walmart a few months later. The prices weren't what we required to make a profit. As a matter of fact, they were 20 percent less. I would have no margin, which would mean I couldn't keep up with the demand or market to build brand awareness.

Immediately I got on the phone. "I'm giving you our lowest price. What's changed?"

"That's not our strategy," the voice said on the other line. "We don't negotiate."

The whole idea was that for EarthKind's product to be in their store, they knew I needed them more than they needed me. They had the upper hand, and I had to play by their rules if I wanted market visibility on their shelves.

It was suggested that I outsource our manufacturing to Mexico to lower our overall cost.

"But our products are grown on farms. We can't go to Mexico," I said, getting more frustrated with their reasoning.

"That's not our problem. We don't negotiate."

"How will I be able to properly manage the quality?"

None of these issues seem to matter to them as long as we

reached the price point. That was their purpose: to have the lowest price for their customer.

Ultimately I had to return to our *why*.

I believe whoever touches our product—from the farmer to the person processing and packaging it—touches it with their energy. I still truly believe that. And on the international production chain, things just kind of go awry. I wanted to know who was growing my stuff, what was in it. And that, to me, was an integrity thing. I had integrity with the EPA, and now I had to continue to have integrity with Walmart. It's true that they could have dramatically grown my business. But they could have dramatically changed it too.

I said no to Walmart, and my people backed me on it. Yes, many people lost out on potential bonuses. But they were proud that I stuck to our principles. We had built this business on a foundation of values, and I wanted to continue to support the farms in America and leave the manufacturing in America as well.

Recently, we had our company party, and we talked about how proud we were of people for speaking up when they felt conflicted with their values or our values. Everyone should have a voice at the table regardless of position. It creates a level playing field. It definitely did not feel like a level playing field when we were negotiating with Walmart.

After I declined to do business with Walmart, I had to face the reality that EarthKind might fail as a company. But the determined farm wife in me, who had worked the land until my hands were dry and cracked so that seedlings could grow and produce fruit, knew that I could work the land of business to provide growth to my seedling of a company.

I was going to prove that we could make it and still keep our values and our principles intact. We weren't going to be another victim of Walmart's profit margin. We were going to be a purveyor of hope in an otherwise ruthless industry. In an ideal world, we would all be able to work together. But for now, we were going to have to go at it alone.

We're going to do this. We *could* do this.

"Hey, Walmart is just one big fish in the sea. There's thousands of others," my bookkeeper said as she went back to her computer, with her usual optimistic attitude.

"You're right. You're absolutely right," I answered, as the others went back to work as if nothing had changed and we didn't just lose a multimillion-dollar account.

It was good to have people like that on my side. People who give you perspective, anchor you to what is important, and encourage you one single step at a time.

There were other fish in the industry sea, and this was a fact that I needed to continually tell myself as much as possible. Yes, Walmart was one of many opportunities and challenges we would face along the road to success. But EarthKind was also one of many choices people would soon be able to make in the pursuit of more ecofriendly options. My only job as one of many ... was to just keep showing up. Keep showing up in this giant sea full of fish and remember that I had just as much right to be here as everyone else did.

13

expansion and the heat of competition

The only source of knowledge is experience.

—ALBERT EINSTEIN

The din of hundreds of voices, mostly male, echoed against the hundred-foot-high ceilings of the Minneapolis Convention Center. I carried in my cases of samples with both arms as I navigated the groups congregating around each booth.

As I opened my box, I surveyed the green tablecloth that hung over the folding table.

It will have to do.

I decided a pyramid would best display the Fresh Cab products I had. I felt excited and full of possibility. There would be 110 attendees, representing 450 doors at that conference—and I was going to sign them all.

I continued to stack my clean brown craft boxes with a colorful handstamp and a picture of a mouse on the front. Not the most professional labeling, but it got the point across.

I heard a man laugh in the booth next to mine. I looked nervously to the right as three men were staring over at me and quickly turned back to their conversation in their professionally designed set up, which easily cost $10,000. I looked to the left. Same thing; another large corporation that was equally as fancy. I was definitely on the cheap and looked like I could have been attending a craft show, not a multimillion-dollar trade show. But I am a farm wife, and I know my product. I was going to save farmers money. I didn't need $10,000 to decorate a booth! My product showcased itself. Especially since everyone could smell it a row away.

Instead of having polypropylene bags to contain the smell of my product, I had polyethylene bags within the cardboard boxes. This meant that the product smell was not contained. If anyone wasn't sure how my products worked, they would know now by the smell.

Looking back, I should have been a bit more prepared. Like a small acorn in a forest of oak trees, I had potential, but no one could see it yet.

After I finished stacking my product, they closed the hall for lunch. I filed out like everyone else, feeling more like cattle than a business mogul. I hung my head as I passed booth after booth of companies who had clearly done this before.

"Yeah," said one of the vendors, "that stuff smells awful, damn vendor with her repellent. I don't know how she even got in here— it looks like she belongs in a flea market. This is bullshit. I'm complaining to the board."

I continued to look down as the hurt welled up inside of me. It was as if the guy doused me with the ice water of reality.

I took a deep breath, shook it off, and took a hard look at what he was really saying. The invisible checklist formed in my head. Yes, the smell was strong. I had to do something about it and switch to bags that would contain the lavender and balsam fir oil. Yes, my booth wasn't as presentable as everyone else's booth, so I needed to invest in some advertising banners. Perception goes far when at a trade show.

At the end of the day, there were two ways to perceive my current situation: as a failure to measure up or an opportunity to rise up. When in doubt, always choose the latter. Your future self will thank you for it.

Toward the end of the day, as I was straightening my tablecloth, the man who made the reality-dousing comments strolled up to me.

"How's business?" he asked with a smirk on his face.

I sighed. This wouldn't be good. But I still chose to be honest.

"Okay, I guess. I signed thirteen accounts, for a total of thirty-five doors." In retail terms, "doors" means the number of locations. I felt shaky inside. Thirty-five doors wasn't even close to what I had wanted to sign.

His eyes widened. "What?" he asked in shock.

It turns out that while thirty-five may have been less than what I expected, it was far more than what he expected.

"Well, I was hoping for all of them."

"You're kidding me," he said, frozen.

"No, there's 450 stores. I need to get all of them. That's why I came here."

"You're unreal," he said shaking his head. "Thirty-five is more accounts than we signed . . . You can't possibly think you can get *all* of them."

"Well, I got thirty-five," I said, standing up straighter to match his height.

He snorted. "Let me see the names." He held out his hand for me to hand over the sign-up sheet.

I turned the clipboard over, and he flipped through the pages slowly. "No frickin' way," he whispered to himself. "That's impossible. Seriously, how is that possible?"

Here was a man with a PhD staring at my wrinkled sign-up sheet, running his hand through his hair in disbelief. To him I was just a farm wife that should have been at a craft show. But here I was, acquiring more accounts than his company projected on their $10,000 budget.

I laugh when I think about his reaction now. He expected that I would fail. He would have bet $1 million on it! But it just proves that if you show up as yourself and believe in yourself, even if you don't have it all ironed out, you can make progress toward achieving your goals. I went home that weekend, signing up thirty-five accounts that would contribute to the growth of EarthKind and leaving behind several naysayers that thought a farm wife wouldn't even sign one.

After that, signing clients picked up speed. I always believed that integrity was the only thing I had when all was said and done. Maybe it was because my father drilled that into me during the hours I spent keeping his financial books from the gas station. I'd seen a few young men my father hired steal, cheat, and lie. I'd find the shortage, and the first time, my father thought it might be me because of a lie told. It wasn't the first time I'd been accused of stealing. It hurt to be accused, but I knew the truth always comes out eventually. I'd watch these kids turn down my father's second chances, like tomorrow didn't exist and their choices didn't define them. I learned early on that being honest, responsible, and hard-working would open far more doors to a young adult's future than trying to get something for nothing today would.

The people buying from you are generally self-employed themselves. A lot of times, like in these farm stores, they know exactly what it takes to be in business. They understand what it's like. One year I decided to call all of the hardware stores to see if they would be interested in carrying our product. Many people hung up on us. Many retailers won't take your calls if your product is not already stocked in their warehouses. Yet, to get into the warehouses, we'd need at least 10 percent of the members buying from us.

"We've got it on special right now. We'll ship it to you for free. If you don't like it 100 percent guarantee, we'll buy it back." This was unheard of at the time because no one was offering to buy back all of their product if it didn't work. You could go out of business! But instead, that was the year we got 10 percent business in every single account with ACE Hardware, True Value, and Do It Best.

Business continued to grow, and as EarthKind got more press, people noticed. I had always known that this was something I was called to do. A farm wife being planted in the soil of the business market. Humble beginnings. Adversity along the way. Reaping what you sow. I was thriving, EarthKind was thriving, and change was happening. We were meeting a need that had never been addressed before, and I felt our company start to hit the tipping point we had been working for.

And with that came new challenges.

One of those challenges was that when the world has an unmet need, many step up. Copycats began to sell similar products to ours, promoting effectiveness and being healthy for our environment. I wish I could say all of them were the real deal, but eventually the true products stood out.

I wasn't shocked or worried when the copycats began to make their way to the market. I expected it. I appreciate and learn from others and respect those who are original. And likewise. We've seen many other products come along, all variations of what I invented. None have done it exactly the way we have done. To date, we still hold the majority of market share, even though we are 30 to 50 percent costlier. Our intent is to always offer the most effective product, with the least burden on the environment, for the best price possible. The customer who buys from us buys for value, not on price. And our customers are loyal to us.

But EarthKind was *only* about the customer.

When I invented Fresh Cab botanical rodent repellent, I got a utility patent. I also got a design patent on the folded pouch. What I did not do, however, was patent the breathable sachet or pouch. With toxic sprays, baits, and toxic granules making up 98 percent of what people were buying and using, I knew that what we had created was a delivery system game-changer. I knew a breathable pouch design was naturally genius and would reduce spray cans filling up our landfills, chlorofluorocarbons polluting our air, and unintended toxins seeping into our water tables from the granular products.

Lift your spirit to a higher place. Open your heart to a kinder earth, and destiny will knock.

I needed to make sure that the "kinder earth" part of my mantra was on my radar even if that meant the intentional decision to give away my hard-earned invention.

It was an ethical decision that would benefit all stakeholders, especially the planet's ecosystems that supported us. I had to meet my competitors where they were. So I made that breathable pouch design open source so anyone could use it. It could be formed, filled, and sealed with traditional food-packaging equipment that was readily available, using feminine pad and baby's diaper materials that were readily available. Everyone could use it, and it benefitted my competitors and the environment, not to mention I was supporting envirofriendly tools.

Business isn't always a friendly banter between competitors. It can be hard and ruthless and exhausting. But there are also moments when a win for one of us is a win for all of us. And inventing this pouch was one of those moments.

But success didn't come without its downfalls. It seldom does. The higher you rise, the more people want to watch you fall. And at the end of the day, humans are humans. And fear can run deep in a human that is feeling threatened for any reason.

There was no end to why some people believed I didn't belong in the industry. Some called me a pot-smoking hippie. Others would laugh at my environmentally ethical principles and think I was a snake oil salesman. Sometimes it was simply because I was a woman. Other times it was because I was thought to not have enough education. Mostly, I was just seen as a farm wife with bigger aspirations that she could handle. There was always something. And there always would be something. Because the issue wasn't who I was or where I came from; the issue was who the other person was and what they were afraid of.

Afraid of competition.

Afraid of accountability.

Afraid of change.

Today, a company is a target no matter what they do. We try to measure ourselves against being a little better each day. Diversity is our greatest competitive advantage as a company. Some people don't dare to be different, but we do. We celebrate our differences and leverage them by understanding one another, including our strengths, weaknesses, goals, and even our communication preferences. It's amazing how liberating it is for people to be given permission to discover their best selves through work. The whole organization prospers when each person is being the contributor they were created to be, doing work that aligns with their values and goals.

When a company does that, and everyone in it has the same growth mindset, business grows faster and with more profit.

But growth can also make a company a target.

I knew I was really good at vision and really good at execution. Together, these two create your billion-dollar companies, your top entrepreneurs, your unique innovators. But where I fall down is alignment.

I knew where the company should go, but the rest of the employees that weren't directly connected to me didn't. It was almost as if I were leading a team of horses but only the back ones knew which direction we were headed.

When a company is smaller, it's much easier. But as you scale, you really have to change how you communicate and articulate and align. In the past, our vision was so coherent. When it was just a few of us, the alignment happened quickly and the team easily adapted. That's why they loved their jobs because everyone knew their place and understood that they were a piece of the bigger puzzle.

Now it takes much longer to get everybody on board.

I have a tendency to go full steam ahead, and I don't stop to celebrate. I don't stop to check to make sure everyone is on board. People can feel alienated under that type of leadership. Not only did I have to meet my team where they were at, but I had to stop and realize I had to meet myself where I was at as a leader. I had to learn how to lead from the table, where everyone had a place to speak.

So that is what I did.

When I was on the farm in the early days, we would have lunch together and we made it a priority to stop and connect. We had that pause. But once I took that away during our growth, it just became much harder to align. So now, whenever we have our company meetings, we always set up a big long table. And we eat together. Actually, our table just keeps getting bigger and bigger as EarthKind continues to grow. Now we've had to wrap it around the warehouse. And I make sure that I move. Seat to seat. Sitting with someone different each time. Because our company wasn't the only thing that had to change and adapt. I did too. We all did. But that change had to start with me. So I sit and I listen.

And I learn.

I'll ask about their kids. I'll find out about their challenges. I'll learn what they are passionate about. I'll know them a little bit more. Serendipity often happens, reminding us that we are right where we need to be.

Maybe it was years in the silence of nature that trained me to use more of my ears than my mouth. Maybe it was the garden that taught me how to make room to grow. Maybe it was storms that taught me to appreciate the stillness.

Every week now, I'll go out for lunch with any employee who wants to. I won't talk much. I'll just listen and eat lunch with them. I have found that there's just something so powerful about it from an alignment standpoint when people know that you care and you listen to their stories.

We meet each other at the table, and maybe we have a bit of lava cake.

14

farm wife to leadership role model

> *You cannot hope to build a better world without improving the individuals. To that end each of us must work for his own improvement, and at the same time share a general responsibility for all humanity, our particular duty being to aid those to whom we think we can be most useful.*
>
> —MARIE CURIE

The jewelry store had the acrid smell of glass cleaner covered up with air freshener. As I made my way to the glass case that held the pearl necklaces, my eyes started to water. You would have thought it was from the cleaner, but it was more than that. Days earlier I received confirmation that I had won the Ernst & Young Entrepreneurial Winning Women Award. It was a big moment for me. This meant that EarthKind and our hard work was being recognized, and I would be joining CEOs at a conference from the top 1 percent of businesses.

Funny thing is, I had never entered a jewelry store except for a wedding band. Life just seldom led me in that direction. But the universe was guiding me to all kinds of new places lately, and this jewelry store was one of them. I ended up buying my first string of pearls and earrings to match. Not the perfectly round pearls, but the more natural kind and long enough that I could circle them or knot them or simply go classic. I was going to get on that plane prepared to accept my inclusion into this elite sisterhood award and, furthermore, this entrepreneurial club, which I felt they had been pushing me out of since the moment I arrived on the scene, as best dressed as I could be.

Winning the EY recognition was transformational to say the least. I didn't realize just *how* transformational it would be until I went to their annual Strategic Growth Forum (SGF) event in Palm Springs, CA. It was like Disney World for enterprising innovative entrepreneurs. EY is the only national and global firm that recognizes entrepreneurs, and let me tell you, they sure know how to throw a great party to celebrate them.

Originally I would resist any type of award or recognition. It felt too ego-driven. Why would I need someone to tell me that Earth-Kind is doing great? I know it was doing great! I could see change happening. Change that EarthKind and the employees had worked together building.

Yet in the business world, award recognition was status quo. It was expected of a business owner to attend these kinds of conferences. And even though I resisted for years, I knew the more you resist things, the harder it is to work through them. And so I allowed myself to step into a new arena, one of dresses, heels, and, yes, pearls.

I stood in front of the bathroom mirror, the fluorescent light glaring over my reflection. The pearls hung in my hand while I stared at them as if ready for battle. I double-looped the strand around my neck, but it hung too loose. I tried to knot them the way the jewelry store attendant told me to, but it didn't look right.

How am I supposed to wear these stupid things?

Some people wear necklaces so incredibly well. Lady Grandma was one of those people. She could tie up a heavy chain of crystals and make it look incredible. But here I was trying to be someone I was not. I thought I was supposed to wear pearls, because that is what you are supposed to do when you win these kinds of things. You have to look the part and follow protocol.

After a few attempts, I got them to hang in what I think was an appropriate fashion. Wearing my white pantsuit and a cotton shirt underneath, I was ready for the afternoon award ceremony.

Minutes later, I wove my way through the crowd of hundreds. I could see security at every door. Decadent treats were at the linen clad tables, the smell of champagne and fresh flowers wafted through the air, and a fountain in the corner overflowed with chocolate, waiting to have a fresh strawberry dipped in its velvety brown liquid.

"Kari! Are we still on for our meeting at three p.m. later today?" a man who is a lobbyist in DC called over to me.

"Yes!" I smiled. My intent was to learn how everything in DC worked and how to really help change policy.

He was just one of many appointments I had during that conference. As a matter of fact, when I emailed my schedule, they told me I had the most meetings set up that weekend. That it might be impossible to have all of those meetings. But I wasn't there just for the chocolate fountain. I had work to do!

One thing I have learned about awards like these is that they can be a mutually beneficial relationship between the giver and the receiver. While at their event, you meet so many people. Others may come up and say, "Hey, I like what you do. Maybe we could get together and discuss what your business is about and see how we can work together." So it's a networking opportunity as well, which in turn allows an entrepreneur to grow their influence.

As I sat down at the table among the other award winners, I took a deep breath. EarthKind had done it. This award meant so much. However, what I didn't realize was that I was partially sitting on the lower strand of my pearls. The tiny misshapen stones dug into my neck, and I felt a lack of air. Shifting slightly to the left, but trying to keep an interested smile on my face as the speaker continued, I tried to adjust the pearls to allow oxygen into my body. No luck.

After a few more attempts, one of which I almost ripped the things off in front of the entire table, the pearls were loosened enough so I could continue the night without dying.

Trying to be someone I'm not was suffocating.

I looked around the room, and I had to say they were all remarkably nice, friendly, warm, compassionate women. They would give you the shirt off their backs, and they were crazy, wickedly smart businesswomen. But one thing that stood out was that I didn't dress like them. They all wore dresses, while I wore a pantsuit. They wore high heels. I wore shoes barely qualified to be heels. I didn't want to fall down the stairs when accepting the award!

gathering around the table

Something about it felt like those moments back in high school all over again, trying to do the right thing and wear the right clothes and say the right words. All just hoping to fit in. It turns out that the desire to belong runs deep in the human spirit. Even when you're an award-winning leader of a game-changing company.

I fought this internal battle as I readied myself to walk on stage. I felt like I had to wear these pearls and dress a certain way. I had to play this game if EarthKind were to take its next step. I knew I had to blend into an industry if I was going to have any impact at all. And damn if it didn't feel uncomfortable.

I heard my name being called over the sound system, and I stood. I concentrated hard on those stairs to make sure I did not trip in front of a crowd of twelve hundred people. But standing up there, gripping onto the silver Tiffany key they had just given me, man, it was something else. I took in the whole room, the hundreds of tables, the mezzanine, huge screens playing a video about EarthKind and what we were all about. Everyone saw that. EarthKind's mission was being awarded.

No one is going to tell you that recognition isn't nice. Especially when it feels like you've had to work twice as hard to get half as far. And because I'm the CEO, I'm the one who receives the recognition when it's handed out. But to me, these awards were—and still are—for my team. When I get one, it's truly for them. It recognizes valiant effort, helps us remember the heartache and joys that got us there and the goals achieved as a result. Transforming ourselves to transform an industry, a team, or a business is hard, pretty much all of the time. It's really about human spirit and bringing our best selves to the now, taking action in faith and trusting each other. Entrepreneurs walk a path that's not yet paved. It's uncharted territory. But they don't do it alone. And neither did I. Building something out of nothing takes extreme leadership and trust within a team to cocreate a new future together. An awards is like a flag in the dirt. We did it! We went to the moon! It has to be captured for our souls, not just our egos.

Once I had accepted the award, I went out to snag a live TV interview. I didn't waste a moment. As I made my way out of the room, I was approached by the director of the winning women. I wasn't sure if I was going to get docked for not wearing heels and a dress, but at least I had the pearls!

"You look stunning!" she said to me. "What a statement to show up in a white suit."

I paused that moment and allowed her words to wash over me. She saw me. She saw me as the person I was and not the person I was trying to be. Most women showed up at these events in red. It was a power color. But it was then that I realized that if I was going to build something reflective of my values, I needed to do so being my most authentic self. Which meant not needing to be like anyone else but myself in order to be a part of this crowd. That standing out isn't necessarily a bad thing. Pearls or no pearls. I soon learned that EY is a role model of diversity and inclusion.

This woman who was the sponsor of the winning women program paused and made sure I knew that standing out as myself was noticed and needed. She gave me permission to show up as Kari, not an imprint of what I thought was expected of me.

After the ceremony and posing for pictures, I went right back to my hotel room. I took those darn pearls off, changed out of the restricting shoes, and went right back to networking. Meeting number one: a potential advisor for EarthKind.

Another meeting I had was with the Kauffman Foundation, which supports education and policy around entrepreneurship. Since meeting them, I have made two videos for them promoting just this, and they have been involving me ever since. And now I was just taking those opportunities and using it for the greater good.

When you're an entrepreneur, oftentimes people can't see your purpose right away. You're trying to sell your vision—this whole new way of doing things—but it isn't seen, so you have to be very inspirational. It's rare that you get awarded for it. It can take years oftentimes to get to the point of being awarded by these kinds of conferences. And then when these opportunities come, it's kind of a different thing. The EY award was business-changing. Because once you put that name behind your name, it's amazing the number of doors that open up. But what stopped me was realizing two things: it was really opening up doors for my employees, and my message for change is where most women fall out. They call it the missing middle for a reason.

The moment I stepped back and allowed these awards to be a tool instead of an obstacle, it helped propel my message and impact forward. When I was lifted up, I realized it lifted everybody else up.

I had no idea how good it would feel to see an employee go from $6.75 an hour to making $70K a year during their time with me. The stories are so rewarding. They are sitting at the table with me, enjoying the fruit of their labor as well. When EarthKind was successful, so were they. When I won an award, it was theirs too.

It was rewarding to see how employees' children believed that anything in life was possible because of what they'd seen from their parents working at EarthKind. It was rewarding to put the entire business in the cloud so employees could have more flexibility with their families and work from home or even their phones. It was rewarding to help my employees gain further education if that's what they wanted.

This business wasn't just about helping myself but helping the lives of those around me as well.

In other words, I didn't want to be the CEO that collects awards for recognition and pulls up in an expensive sports car, while my employees can't afford gas. Maybe it's because I've already died once. It has a way of giving you perspective.

And yet, I had to learn that recognition is about lifting up those around you. And the younger generation can see that. They reward authenticity, rightfully so. I didn't want to be that old leader that has all the awards, all of the fanfare that goes with it, that builds them up, and yet I had to struggle with accepting the recognition, that in the frame of mind of using it for good, it could be a gift. That feedback can be so incredibly valuable to people who are looking to join forces to do business with each other.

Going home on the plane after the conference, I felt immense satisfaction. I had spoken with many women from different backgrounds, and I realized we all had something in common: we were not afraid to rock the boat of the business world, we were not afraid to be bold for a cause that we believed in.

As a matter of fact, our attending and accepting these awards wasn't about how smart we were or how attractive we were, what shoes we wore, or how we wore our pearls. It was more about our ability to bring bigger thinking to one another. We had big plans, plans that shape markets, keep economies going, accountants employed, and capital rolling. I developed quality relationships with those ladies, and in doing so, I took those pearls off and was able to be me.

Years later, I can look at the EY conference attendees and see other women showing up as themselves. There is no pressure on a specific type of person being accepted. We have made it known that we all have common ground that we are tilling to plant the seeds. All we had to do was give each year's new class permission to be themselves like the director of EY Winning Women did for me years ago.

A few days after the conference, the warmth of the mid-afternoon sun tickled my toes. I was sitting on the floor with my legs stretched out in front of me, going through paperwork for my meeting with a new customer that I had met at the EY conference. My pearls were around my neck tied in a small knot that complemented the simple t-shirt and jeans that I wore. Because I had learned that I didn't need to be them in order to be successful, but I didn't need to shy away from their game either.

I could wear pearls my way. And I could do business my way too. I felt like Lady Grandma would be proud.

15

conscious capitalism: power of community

We need red blood cells to live, the same way a business needs profits to live, but the purpose of life is more than to make red blood cells, the same way the purpose of business is more than simply to generate profits.

—R. Edward Freedman and Ellen R. Auster

"Let's go sit up front so we can see the real show," the man with the wild brown hair suggested. He had just won the 500/5000 award for the fifteenth year in a row at this conference, and now he was nudging me with his elbow to get a better view. "I'll let you use my wife's badge so they'll let you up there."

I nodded with a grin. I wondered why it took only fifteen years of winning the same award to be allowed to sit up front at the good tables. There was a hierarchy here, a pecking order so to speak. The more I earned, the more places I was allowed.

We arrived at the head table and sat down. As I looked around, I noticed two women whispering and looking over at me. My face was displayed on the big screen as one of the award winners, so she must have recognized me. I smiled and she returned one.

Her counterpart didn't look too pleased. She whispered something to her, and she quietly looked down.

Are you kidding me? Are they not going to talk to me?

I waited for a break between speakers so I could approach the women, and moments later we were having a lovely conversation together. I could see the spark in one woman's eyes. I built a woman-owned business. Encouraging one another is important to me.

The woman with the eye spark opened and shut her mouth several times. I could see she was aching to say something, but something was stopping her.

"Do you want to say something to me. Because I am here, you can say it," I said with an encouraging smile.

"I . . . I think it is very promising to see what you are doing," she softly told me.

"How so?"

"Because to see a woman up there receiving an award and to see what you've created . . . I think it's very promising."

The other woman swiftly nudged her under the table while she suddenly fell silent and looked the other way. I was shunned. Quite literally, not welcome at their table. But then again, I had come to learn over the years that most of our industry believed in building higher fences instead of longer tables. You had to earn your way to the front of the room. You had to know the right people and do the right things and win the right awards.

It felt a lot like the high school cheerleading team all over again.

I sincerely tried not to say anything, but I just couldn't help it. I leaned very close to the colleague and said loud enough for all to hear, "I just wanted you to know you're both amazing things. It's an honor to be here with you."

If I was going to be rejected from the table ... then I was at least going to leave being the bigger person.

The awards went on that night, people being recognized for how fast their company grew and how much money they made, but I didn't hear anything about community, purpose, or values. It was funny. Even though I was at one of the most important tables, I didn't feel a part of it. There was no connection with what I truly believed and hoped to achieve. I felt disillusioned.

And many conferences are like this: a place for entrepreneurs to come together and celebrate each other's financial successes. A place to stand upon our ivory towers and recognize how high we've risen. It's why leadership can be such a lonely place, because we aren't encouraged to connect through purpose and values. We are encouraged to compete through profit and power. And when that's not the race you are wanting to run, you naturally end up feeling more alone.

Because the ceremony felt like a huge letdown, even when sitting at the head table, I decided to never apply again. It felt cold and devoid of anything I'd learned about servant leadership in my own journey to becoming a fast-growing business. The words "purpose," "soul's desire," "North Star," or "humanity" weren't used. I felt pain for the chaos the thousands of employees must have faced during such periods of rapid growth. I wanted to hear the lessons learned, but instead I got lip service. There wasn't a community other than those leading it. It felt like the complete opposite of "Lift your spirit to a higher place, open your heart to a kinder earth." I knew there needed to be a network somewhere that valued "why" business was done and not just "how much" of it was being done.

Cue Conscious Capitalism.

Near the end of that year, I took one of my usual walks through nature to unearth what my company theme would be for the next twelve months. It felt good to listen to the wind and breath in the winter air as I focused my prayer. I quieted my mind and listened.

A cardinal chirped to my left, and I saw it hopping from one snowy branch to the other. I took another deep breath and let that sound fade into my being, as if there might be a message there.

You need to change your networks.

A strong intuition weighed on me. I glanced around as I half smiled. *What? Networks?* I half laughed but accepted it as I continued my walk.

Weeks later, I got a call from my friend who considered herself to be a Conscious Capitalist, a leader who was determined to use her business for the betterment of everyone around her. She knew that I was looking for something new, and she had an extra ticket for a conference she was attending in Austin with her husband.

"I think it would be really good for our country and our community if you would go," her husband said to me.

I listened intently to what they said, the enormity of it all, because I had just watched them give $1 million to a local charity the week before and had great respect for their commitment to community.

162

Opening myself up to the possibility that this may be the new network I was looking for, I accepted the invitation and came with expectancy.

The first morning of the conference, I woke up to the sounds of horses whinnying and the smell of the expanse of land. The sun made its rosy appearance from the east, and I let it warm my face as I stood on the balcony of my room.

I glanced to my right and saw one of the conference attendees practicing Qigong on one of the many lawns. To my right, there was a group of people doing early morning runs. In the distance, a few other people were on mats practicing yoga.

I smiled as I pulled out my internal checklist and thought, "Oh, this network is definitely a possibility."

But what struck me more was what was the discussion throughout the entire conference.

How do we evolve policy?

How do we evolve educational systems?

How do we evolve business?

Everything was intersecting in a community-based way. Everyone was equal, and you didn't need a badge to access a table at the front. We all were invited to the same table. The environment supported the whole self—body, mind, and soul. There were outdoor tents with comfy furniture for those who wanted to break away and have real conversations around purpose, transparency, policy, and structuring stock for protection when going public. The food was organic, and there was no hard alcohol being consumed that I could see. There was no criticizing, condemning, and complaining like I'd heard at other conferences—even from the speakers. The meeting rooms were even set up like a huge living room, with couches and chairs and tables and living walls of plants. Love sacs lined the halls for the ultimate getaway to check messages. There was an infrastructure of community being built here. And the foundation was one of values, purpose, and service to others.

But the moment that tipped everything for me that weekend was when one of the speakers discussed a book about how insects team up.

I gasped. *Oh, this is definitely my tribe.*

From that retreat on, I was all in! I've attended every annual conference since and loved them all. I always seemed to bring home a better self, which I pay forward to all my coworkers.

This community also helped me voice what I truly believed. I had always practiced being a Conscious Capitalist but didn't have the tribe to walk with and hold me accountable to my own growth and direction. The tenets of Conscious Capitalism resonated with my soul while giving me a community to grow alongside.

This community believed in a **Higher Purpose**. One of our core values at EarthKind is faith. Faith means we believe in our North Star, as individuals and as a company. It's a conscious recognition of our higher purpose. It's the "why" that fulfills us and puts the universe to work aligning the resources on our behalf when we are consciously aware of it. I don't think it was a coincidence that the mantra "Lift your spirit to a higher place. Open your heart to a kinder earth, and destiny will knock" is something that will forever be part of my DNA as it spills out into the way I do business.

This community believed the importance of **caring for**

everyone in their ecosystem, motivating their stakeholders by creating winning outcomes for all who are impacted by their business. If I could have shouted this from the treetops, I would have. EarthKind was exactly this. We wanted our employees to win. We wanted our farmers and suppliers to win. We wanted our customers to win. We wanted the environment to win. We wanted the pests to win (by not being killed), and I even set my competition up to win by providing the free invention of the breathable bags and market leadership without market-controlled ownership.

A sales guy once asked me why EarthKind was so nice to him. I shared that we were concerned with his safety and his home after the deluge of rain that happened while he was visiting our plant to meet a deadline. He told me he'd applied for a job after using our products. He really was confused about how we would take time to care. Like we're not human because we're in business. We believe kindness is like a boomerang: it always returns.

This community believed that a **conscious leader must focus on "we" rather than me**. They inspire transformation and bring out the best in those around them.

One of the employees at EarthKind has been with us for eight years. She has brought her baby to work at times. She is part of our family. One night we were at a table eating dinner together, and she said something so profound to me.

"You know, Kari, I don't know if I will ever quit because I've had so much opportunity here. I'm able to help my mother who runs her own business. I've saved my family because of what I've learned."

I set down my fork and folded my hands. "What do you mean?"

"Sure, I've learned how to run a business, but it's more than that.

I've also learned how to have a conversation, how to deal with conflict, and how to widen my perspective with others even if I don't understand where they are coming from."

Leading is simply a matter of influencing others.

And last, this community believed that the **culture of a business is its heartbeat**. It fosters love and care for all stakeholders involved. It also includes accountability, transparency, integrity, loyalty, egalitarianism, fairness, and personal growth, acting as an energizing and unifying force that truly brings a conscious business to life. This is coming directly from their tenets, and I couldn't have said it better myself!

I've seen how our teams that fire together wire together. By this, I mean that our neural networks as individuals—and as a company—develop in tandem by opening our hearts to our purpose, marching to the same heartbeat, and using our brains in support of our mission. We learn and grow together. Even the communities we live and work in are transformed as a result. You've heard that we become the sum of our five closest friends. Well, it's like that. I think business done in this way will be the norm one day, because it's truly possible to make money without doing so at the expense of one (or more) stakeholders that always get the short end of the stick, like I'd so often seen in farming. Rather, it means doing business as a conscious leader, cocreating a better way to do business, utilizing the collective intelligence of all stakeholders.

We've had companies we work with update their culture based on what they experienced working with us. They had never witnessed the level of excellence they found at EarthKind, the ease of working with a company, the innovative collaboration, and such a strong purpose. Our little company changed the future of the second-largest fragrance house in the world. After they saw the market-defying growth we had, they looked closer and met as a board. They decided to become more like us. I was humbled when told this, but it's not the first time. It happens. Repeatedly.

For many people, capitalism is a dirty word. To me, capitalism works. Its power to positively change lives is unparalleled. Sadly, the misuse of capitalism's power by some has led to negative stereotypes such as greed, collusion, and exclusion. Yes, some people do business this way. Too many people, even. But what's important to recognize is that it's not the *only* way to do business. For generations, it seemed unlikely that our industry would break free from this unshakable narrative—until now. There is a better way to be a capitalist. A way that will create a better world for everyone. A way forward for humankind to liberate the heroic spirit of business and our collective entrepreneurial creativity so we can be free to solve the many social, environmental, political, and economic challenges we face. Conscious Capitalism provides that path.

Right now there is about $21 billion missing from the economy. If you put every business person in the room and gave them a red button to stop business and hold what they've got, or a green button to go for it and continue to invest, most people would choose the red button. They're going to choose the safe option because their pension funds are tied to the status quo, their retirements are tied to it, and their livelihoods are tied to it. But then there's the other option, and I believe that the Conscious Capitalism movement is an emergent way of pushing the green button because it doesn't have to be all or nothing. We can move the economy to

167

where money flows, and we make enough of it that we don't have to compromise. Money and good can go together.

While sitting at the table for breakfast with some highly successful ladies at the most recent Conscious Capitalism retreat, I noticed a friend of mine, a woman who invented and patented a way to eliminate poverty. She's been out in Africa, working in villages and bringing in their handmade baskets to retailers—a total dynamo. Her family came from bootleggers, and she grew up in poverty, her brothers toting sawed-off shotguns to ward off the law that would come after them. It made me chuckle when I looked at all of us, some having come from old money, some paving the way on our own, but all gathering together because we belonged.

"Teresa!" I called, waving my hand. "Come sit with us."

She nodded, made her way over, and set her plate on the wooden table, her fork clattering as it spilled from her napkin.

She held out her calloused hands to one of the women. "Teresa," she introduced herself.

The stark difference between the two was apparent to me: one had perfectly manicured hands, the other worked in the dirt all her life.

And right there was the very essence of what Conscious Capitalism stands for: the idea that there is no "right" way to do business as long as we are doing it with heart and soul and purpose. Manicured nails behind a desk impacts just as much change as being knee-deep in the mess of what's happening an entire continent away. We aren't here to compare, to judge, to be like anyone else. We are here to make a difference in our own unique ways.

At Conscious Capitalism, everyone has a seat at the table.

16

locking arms with changemakers

When you tug at a single thing in nature, you find it attached to the rest of the world.

—JOHN MUIR, PIONEERING NATURALIST

One of the things I do as CEO is to form win-win relationships with other leaders whose purposes are aligned with my own. It's called **locking arms**. It's systematic and it's strategic and it's one of the biggest jobs of an industry leader and changemaker.

It's an amazing occurrence when people weave their own story into the storyline of what's happening around them. Things magically come together. When we choose to join forces, we've set the groundwork to make that happen.

It's as if you are going to a potluck, and everybody brings something to the table to share.

When you choose to work together, each person's unique perspective brings a new facet to an idea. But we all must participate together. Everyone needs to be thinking in the same direction because to me, innovation is a brain activity that can ignite radical change when connected to purpose.

I've watched it happen, and the sheer force of its potential has never failed to amaze me.

During one particular event, I was invited to DC. The government asked each state to send two representatives to participate in a roundtable of innovative brainstorming. We were placed in teams of eight to ten people, gathered together, throwing out ideas to solve some of our country's most pressing issues. They gave us projects to work on, and we found the gateway to creativity was just to begin by talking it out.

One particular project had us addressing the issue of illegal activity in the waterways. There was too much to handle, and the law enforcement couldn't catch most of what was going on. They were simply spread too thin.

"Maybe there's something we could put under the water to track the new boats," one of our group members suggested.

"Maybe we could use a satellite," another chimed in.

"You know, the Israeli intelligence still uses the old-fashioned techniques of trusting their eyes and their feelings."

"This is true. We rely so much on machines, and here the Israelis have caught so many people using human intelligence."

This conversation sparked an idea for me. Using human intelligence rather than machines. What humans are near the waterways the most? *Fishermen.*

"What if we deputize fishermen?" I asked.

The excitement of our idea was palpable as the reasoning

developed. Deputizing resident fishermen to watch for illegal activities was a great idea because the fishermen are in the waterways every day. They know that environment intimately, some even growing up on the waterway because fishing is a family business. They would know when something is not right. The fisherman can earn some extra money, the waterways are safer, law enforcement isn't spread so thin, and you have all hands on deck. It was a brilliant solution, and we came with it by changing the perspective of who can watch.

Problem solved.

But it couldn't be solved alone.

Innovativeness to me is utilizing the differences that we all have and looking at things in a different way. Asking different questions and being open to different answers. It's problem-solving at its finest, and it breaks down silos and learned behaviors that no longer serve us. I love being in business, especially manufacturing, because it provides a table for every section of the economy to sit, from the farmers who grow our ingredients to policy to the 90 percent in between that makes up our communities.

However, being an innovator means more than just your own great ideas. You have to let go of all attachment to things. When little kids play, normally they aren't worried so much about being accepted; they just play, and the creativity happens. It's the same with being an innovator: you let go of all worry about acceptance and what others perceive about you, and you just let the magic happen by seeing things in new ways, which happens with an open heart.

It's such a privilege to watch what everyone is capable of bringing to the table.

And it's also a privilege to be invited to have a seat at another entrepreneur's table.

Geena Davis has been gracing movie screens as an American icon for over three decades. She's best known for her portrayal of strong female characters, and what many people don't know is that she is an even stronger female force off the screen. I didn't know this either. Until she offered me the opportunity to sit down at the table one day. She invited me to speak on a panel at the Bentonville film festival in 2018, and since then I've had the unique privilege of getting to know her in a more personal way. Gina singlehandedly moved the dial on equality in cinema over the past fifteen years, a milestone that was finally reached in 2020, as filmmakers cast the characters that the public wanted. The Geena Davis Institute helped make this happen, through research, through advocacy, through innovation.

I have so much respect for this woman that it's not even funny. She has become a mentor and someone I look up to. I sincerely hope to be as graceful as her one day. She's truly an angel in person and so frickin' smart. She is the very definition of *locking arms* across industry.

During these forums, I learned that consumer products are the top influencer for social change, by which I mean they are hugely powerful agents for social impact. I think back to how that little girl on the shampoo bottle made me feel "less than pretty" when I was five. This fact has helped me hold firm to my purpose at Earth-Kind. You empower one home at a time, and over time—twenty years in my case—the earth becomes a little kinder.

I have a vision for the future that includes our fellow leaders making the choice to use their powers for good and not evil. It's Conscious Capitalism. It's taking a position of influence and using that to make the world a better place. It's about replacing the question "What is this going to get me?" with "How can we use the tools of influence to help each other and the world around us?"

Later, Geena introduced me to John Paul DeJoria of Paul Mitchell Systems, and, oh my gosh, I really liked that guy.

The streets were golden from the sun beginning its descent in the late afternoon, and he and I got a chance to talk about business and I learned so much.

The average tenure of his employees is twenty-two years. *Twenty-two.*

One of his biggest beliefs is that women have been lied to. He believes that generations and generations of lies have been fed to us, telling us that we are powerless. But he said, "You've always had the power. You just need somebody to remind you. And that's what I do; I remind women that they've always had the power."

He has helped former drug runners in Mexico work in a thriving tequila business.

He has hired people who were previously poachers of seals to now protect them in larger, faster boats.

After our afternoon walk, I felt more inspired than ever to use everything I had to help others. And I wouldn't have met him if I hadn't met Geena.

It's locking arms with other conscious leaders.

It's locking arms with retailers who hold the same values.

It's locking arms with the government to be on an advisory board to ensure entrepreneurs and women get help.

It's locking arms with the Dale Jr. Foundation and other local groups to help families in need.

It's locking arms with new entrepreneurs to help mentor them.

It's locking arms with universities about conscious leadership.

It's locking arms with my sisterhood of EY Entrepreneurial Winning Women and supporting each other.

And at the end of the day, the sum of all our parts is equal to the whole.

We have a responsibility as leaders to make that whole as strong as possible and to find people that will both encourage us and hold us accountable all at the same time. Leadership is a privilege, not a right. It must be held sacredly.

What's interesting about finding all of these people and organizations to lock arms with is that you also find this common ground, common purpose, common values. It's a camaraderie that reminds me very much of breaking bread with somebody. The barriers fall away, humanity shines through, the weight becomes lighter. And it becomes a reciprocal thing. You give and then you get.

We all get to serve each other when we've got a seat at the table.

17

the conversation

There is no power for change greater than a community discovering what it cares about.

—Margaret J. Wheatley

The scent of caramel and medium roast coffee wafted in the air the minute I opened the door to the coffee shop. I was meeting a girl from one of the local colleges in town. I had spoken in her business class a couple of weeks earlier, and then she reached out to see if she could ask a few more questions. I was beyond happy to oblige. A few minutes later I snagged a spot by the window, a tiny table with two oversized chairs. I enjoy watching the people that pass by. It's always entertaining, you know, to see who is in a hurry and who is just enjoying the bright sunny day.

"Kari?" The barista called out, signaling my oatmeal with walnuts and a dash of cinnamon and real maple syrup was ready along with a cup of chamomile tea. I knew it was unusual to have tea in this place, but then again, I don't order according to what is "usual."

A few minutes later, I saw my guest walk in. She had long dark hair and she was pretty, athletic, and clean cut. As a matter of fact, most of the kids that ask me for coffee are seldom ever flashy. They come in wearing sneakers, jeans, button-up shirts. No fragrances, no heavy makeup. No flashy logos on their clothes. As kids of small business owners like ranchers, undertakers, or hairdressers, they've usually grown up serving others in church and the community. They sell popcorn balls at the school to pay for prom decorations. They put together the yearbooks or plan the graduation ceremony. They serve in FFA, 4H, or Boy Scouts.

The time when people find their purpose in entrepreneurship generally has been at college, or they hear an inspiring speech from those that have gone before them. Sometimes people come up and tell me, "Oh my gosh, I decided to become an entrepreneur!" At this inflection point, they are making a decision and trying to find someone to light the path forward, which is part of EarthKind's purpose as a company and what we're doing in the industry. And of course, this was something that was also done for me as I grew in leadership. Helping another discern direction, a new path forward, is one those things that I've always felt passionate about when it comes to new entrepreneurs. Today was no different.

She sat down with a small coffee in her hand and smiled sheepishly. "Thank you for meeting me, Mrs. Block. I just wanted to let you know that I see my servant leadership values through you. When you were talking at our college the other day . . . I just, well, it was so great."

I returned her smile. It tends to ignite a spark within them when they hear of a different way to do business. A purpose-driven way of doing business, of being able to live through servant leadership rather than through the ways of the world.

"Thank you. I wanted to let you know that I am here for you and rooting for you. We all need a little of that."

"Thank you," she whispered.

"So you have some questions?" I asked as I pointed to her oversized laptop bag. "What are you gonna do, write an entire article!?"

She laughed. "Just helps me not forget what I wanted to ask. I've been so excited for a week since you said you'd meet with me." She pulled out her laptop and opened it up. With tiny clicks of her keyboard, the screen flashed on her face, illuminating her smile as she looked up nervously.

"I am happy to answer any questions you have," I said with a warm smile. Usually most of the kids that meet me for mentorship are nervous and excited. Like bubbles coming up to the surface of a pot about to boil over. They don't realize that I'm really just like them. Still a perfectly imperfect human, just hoping to make a difference in the world.

"Well . . . I ugh. I don't know where to start. How do I know what step to take in being an entrepreneur?"

"You should start small and let each step guide you to the next." She typed vigorously as I continued. "And learn to trust God to do the rest."

She looked up from her computer and scratched her chin. "What if I make the wrong choice?"

I laughed. Of course I knew the consequences of making wrong choices. Don't we all? "Just keep showing up and be consciously present. Which is harder than anything to do. When we do that, even a misstep will lead us back to the right path. If we keep our heart set on what we are envisioning and use our minds in service to that, it will attract it. Like attracts like—that's how it works."

"When you started out, you sold potpourri. How did you know when to switch to Fresh Cab?"

I stirred my oatmeal much like the way Lady Grandma would do when we sat down at the table during our early morning conversations. "You know, it's never a straight path. Mine wasn't. Find a problem that needs solving. A problem that you might be uniquely qualified to solve better than anyone else can. When we sell something that is needed, people who have the money to buy, will. Do it in a way that's kind to the earth and feels like your destiny." She and I both laughed at "kind to the earth."

She scrolled through her notes and then looked back up at me. "Mrs. Block, how can you go through so much and be so calm? I mean, you had so many people say no to EarthKind. People made fun of you. You even got shut down by the EPA!"

I laughed. Smart girl. She had done her research. I love it when these kids come prepared with the tough questions!

"It's the 'breaking down' of a person that prepares them to be built back up. Stronger than ever. After we are broken down, we realize it's much like evolution—the flow of nature. All things transform through fire, pain, and need, basically. We can either resist it, or we can learn to accept it as it is, which is rarely how we think it is. I've come to trust that it's all as it's supposed to be and that it all works in the end."

"Well wait, how do you forgive and forget all the things people say and do to successful businesses like EarthKind?"

I stirred my oatmeal a bit more, a little splashing on the wooden table with a few nicks in the finish. "This question you ask is about disillusion. I had to learn to let go of emotion in healthy ways. I had to let go of 'coulda shoulda woulda' in my vocabulary. I reflect, I journal, I ground myself in the earth, I exercise it off. I think of it like cleansing, purifying. I tell myself all people are good, divine. They may not be acting like it at this moment, so forgive them. They may not always realize what they are doing. I hope they'll do the same for me if I am at a low time in my life."

The girl smiled at me. "What kind of exercise?"

I laughed because I could see that she was wondering what I did at my age. "Well, it's not jazzercise! Yoga is my go-to."

She giggled. I enjoyed seeing her excitement to change the world in her own way. It was such a grown-up thing to do, and yet her giggling reminded me that she was still young. It's life though. Needing to bring the younger generation up to be authentic, real, and passionate about their purpose. They aren't given a fair shot when it comes to business. When it comes to entrepreneurship. But they can if we have gone before them, help them, like reaching a hand back behind us on our paths. Like those who did the same for me.

"How did you get people to believe in your idea, when the current reality says the exact opposite? I mean, lots of people struggle to believe—especially younger people such as myself because we don't have the experience!"

I sighed and patted her arm because I know what unbelief can do to a person. "Listen, this question is about vision and leadership.

Here's what I can tell you about selling your vision: Shared hardship creates oxytocin. Yes, the 'feel-good hormone.' We are wired for this. People want to do good, and it makes them feel good if you can connect them to that by taking action to help. I always look for the pain, or the fear, and connect to that when selling the vision. At EarthKind, we offer a natural solution—'peace and harmony'—around pest control rather than doom and gloom. Yes, not everyone's buying it, but those who do feel it get shivers, and they know they were meant to follow. I personally love taking some of the pain out of the way of farmers dealing with chewed-up wiring and mouse mess. I've been there. I know that frustration and cost."

"So shared pain equals shared vision?" she asked, furrowing her eyebrows. This was the stuff of conversations for growth!

"Exactly! I don't think any of life is a coincidence. That pain that we, or someone we care about, is experiencing is also leading to something we need to heal in ourselves or the world. As an entrepreneur, I decided not to picket or protest what I hated. Instead, I decided to follow the loving path. Which meant to create a naturally smarter solution that made it easy to be kind to nature's delicate ecosystems when controlling pests."

A few more people filed into the shop while the whir of the espresso machine drowned out their conversation. She continued clicking away at those last sentences as I sipped my tea. It was these conversations that I lived for, pouring into the minds of young entrepreneurs. And seeing the excitement when they "get it." Their purpose. It's the stuff of life.

"Okay ... two more questions," she said while her coffee was left untouched for the last twenty minutes. I can always tell those that are soaking everything in, because they forget about their coffees. "How do you incorporate your values?"

"Hmm, that is a good one. I make sure that all my decisions align with my ethics and morals as an individual. For instance, innovation. I run EarthKind as a zero-carbon footprint company because I don't want to contribute to what I saw as a young girl at the Kills Dump. It requires collaborative and innovative efforts from artists, educators, policy makers, scientists, and farmers to make it happen. Compassion is another big one. Most people don't know what that truly means. It's passion in action. Compassion doesn't mean playing 'nice' like the monkeys do in the jungle, playing nice so they don't get beat up. That's manipulation. Compassion is about taking action toward what you are passionate about, using that 'force' to build the world you'd love to live in versus a world we hate. The third is excellence, which is simply showing up each day, doing your best, and not making unproductive comparisons to anyone or anything other than your own best. The last is faith. It's following your own North Star and encouraging others around you to do the same. Faith is the most powerful of all, because when we're aware and respectful of one another's uniqueness as individuals, it facilitates conscious connections any place you go. It's like turning on your light switch for the angelic realm. What you want starts coming to you, often with a lesson to learn and others to help. At EarthKind, we see it every day and call it 'kismet.' And it's truly magical when you see it for what it is. These are all things I value and therefore work on twenty-four seven. That's why it's incorporated into my life at home, work, and play."

"Okay, last question: when did you know you'd made it?"

I nodded. Most of the kids that interviewed me ask this one. "When I won the EY Winning Women award in 2012. I realized I made it to the EY class of 2012 not because of what I looked like, where I lived, what I drove, or who I knew. I made it there on my wits, my courage, my tenacity, and convincing others to believe in my vision. It's like the wheat separating from the chaff at harvest. While together, I doubt they realized there were two parts. I saw a new truth about myself after that. I saw me through the other winning women, and I liked it. I became bolder, and I started to think bigger as a result of getting out of my own way. At that point, I knew I could sell out or keep going. Even though the cash wasn't in the bank, it was in the 12x valuation of what I built from my vision. I decided to keep going. The money was a current of energy to accomplish our mission, not a way out. I knew I had made it when I could wear the pearls and still feel like myself."

"Wait, the pearls?" she asked.

"Oh, nothing . . . that's a story for another time," I told her, smiling out the window as I thought about the strand that I continued to wear every now and then.

After she typed for another few minutes and I scraped the last of the oatmeal from the bowl, she closed her laptop.

"Mrs. Block, I wanted to tell you that I appreciate you so much. I can't wait to tell my parents what we spoke about today."

"Listen," I said as she finally remembered her coffee and took a sip. "It's not easy. You will run into all these hard things that no one in their right mind would want to do as an entrepreneur. It's a tough job. Nobody may want to take you seriously at first. Stay true to your values. And no matter what is said about you, be kind anyway."

She grinned as she stuffed her laptop in her bag and grabbed her now empty cup of coffee. "Thank you, Mrs. Block. I'll call you if I have any more questions."

She stood up, and I watched her toss her cup into the recycling bin and push the door open, letting the sunshine give a full blast to her face. Instead of squinting, she closed her eyes and smiled.

I took a sip of my chamomile tea and ran my hand over the highly polished table before me. How many conversations like this one had I participated in at a table? Twenty? One hundred? The flat surface seemed as if it were pulling me into the recesses of my memory of all the moments where my life had changed when I was invited to a table.

At Kills Dump where I saw women peddling their wares found in the trash pile, and I learned that the earth was worth fighting for.

When Lady Grandma would eat her oatmeal, and we would talk about anything, everything, and it made me feel whole.

During the earliest days of EarthKind when we were still just a small business—working from the farm, making lunch for them, and eating around the worktable—and I felt community.

At my square brown kitchen table where I spent the early morning hours learning how to present to the big-name stores, and my purpose found a voice.

When I talked with Jim for hours at a little bar tabletop, and we began to fall in love.

When Jim and I ate lava cake and I received a call telling me that we had won the fight with the EPA, and my determination gave EarthKind a place.

At our company-wide lunches where we gather together to find support and offer encouragement.

At a circular table with a crisp white linen cloth decorated with flowers as I waited for my EY Winning Women award and learned to be myself.

And now at this table, having coffee with the next generation of entrepreneurs to help them in their journey so they can find their purpose.

I invite you to this table. Where change happens. Where you can go and find your purpose, break bread with others. Where you learn more about people you didn't know before just by eating with them. Where we express anything that our souls want to share. Where everyone has a voice. Where human connection happens. Where we can lift our spirits to a higher place, open our hearts to a kinder earth, find our purpose and break the bread.

Because at the end of the day, there is nothing like celebrating at a table with those around you. And having a little bit of lava cake afterward.

acknowledgments

This book wouldn't have come into its form without my editor and writers Gen, Mary Anna, and Sarah. Every meeting we had took us on a magical carpet ride, a journey mapped on paper in such a way that the readers would feel 110 percent empowered to do the impossible, to do the improbable, to be builders of human spirit, and to be protectors of natural resources through the heroic spirit of business. It's time to rebuild and reinvent everything as we know it.

I also wanted to say "thank you" to everyone who's lifted me up in so many ways; the leadership lessons I learned from them, the connections I've made through them, the doors opened by them, the doors shut by them. I don't think I could possibly name them all: the church ladies, teachers, employers, employees, friends, family, trading partners, scientists, bankers. Every person I've ever met has been part of my life's journey.

Lastly, my kids and husband to whom I am grateful that they continue to love me, support me, and think it's cool that I'm weird.

acknowledgments for epigraphs

Chapter 4

Fukuoka, Masanobu. *The One-Straw Revolution: An Introduction to Natural Farming*. Translated by Larry Korn, Chris Pearce, and Tsune Kurosawa. Edited by Larry Korn. New York: New York Review of Books, 2009.

Chapter 7

Sarton, May. *The Journals of May Sarton Volume One: Journal of a Solitude, Plant Dreaming Deep, and Recovering*. New York: Open Road Media, 2017.

Chapter 10

Wilson, Woodrow. *The Politics of Woodrow Wilson: Selections from His Speeches and Writings*. Edited with an introduction by August Heckscher. New York: Harper & Brothers, 1956.

Nietzsche, Friedrich. *Twilight of the Idols*. In *Twilight of the Idols and The Anti-Christ*. Translated by R. J. Hollingdale, 33. London: Penguin, 1990.

Chapter 11

Eliot, George. *Adam Bede*. Edited by Mary Waldron. Toronto: Broadview Press, 2005.

Chapter 14

Curie, Marie. *Pierre Curie: With Autobiographical Notes by Marie Curie*. Translated by Charlotte and Vernon Kellogg. New York: Macmillan, 1923.

Chapter 15

Freeman, R. Edward, and Ellen R. Auster. *Bridging the Values Gap: How Authentic Organizations Bring Values to Life*. Oakland, CA: Berrett-Koehler Publishers, 2015.

about the author

An inspirational public speaker, nature lover, and author, Kari Warberg Block was the first to educate the public on how to keep their homes pest- and poison-free without paying a hefty price, personally or environmentally. Once a farmer and now CEO of EarthKind, a manufacturer of naturally powerful and effective insect and rodent deterrents, she cultivated the fastest-growing household pest prevention brand and only pest control brand that considered the health and well-being of all stakeholders—including the pests. Kari is a former member of the NWBC, which advises the president, the US Small Business Administration, and the United States Congress on matters of impact and importance for women in business. On her personal blog *One of a Kind*, Kari shares insightful discoveries made along her entrepreneurial journey as the leader of EarthKind and her passion for serving others. Underneath her words, you'll find a soul that consciously cares for the well-being of the planet and all its inhabitants. Kari lives in North Carolina with her husband Jim and their rescue dog Benny on a little corner of the earth she is happy to call her own and share with the local wildlife.

ELEVATE HUMANITY THROUGH BUSINESS.

Conscious Capitalism, Inc., supports a global community of business leaders dedicated to elevating humanity through business via their demonstration of purpose beyond profit, the cultivation of conscious leadership and culture throughout their entire ecosystem, and their focus on long-termism by prioritizing stakeholder orientation instead of shareholder primacy. We provide mid-market executives with innovative learning exchanges, transformational storytelling training, and inspiring conference experiences all designed to level-up their business operations and collectively demonstrate capitalism as a powerful force for good when practiced consciously.

We invite you, either as an individual or as a business, to join us and contribute your voice. Learn more about the global movement at www.consciouscapitalism.org.

CPSIA information can be obtained
at www.ICGtesting.com
Printed in the USA
LVHW080827230321
681668LV00101B/1815/J